Music and dancing at Castletown, County Kildare, 1759–1821

Karol Mullaney-Dignam

7 Dec 2011

Maynooth Studies in Local History

SERIES EDITOR Raymond Gillespie

This volume is one of six short books published in the Maynooth Studies in Local History series in 2011. Like their predecessors they range widely, both chronologically and geographically, over the local experience in the Irish past. That local experience is presented in the complex and contested social worlds of which it is part. As such they reflect the divide between popular beliefs about women healers in Kildare and the music and dancing in a great house in the same county, the military confrontations of revolutionary Galway and the legal confrontations of breach of promise cases in Limerick and the differing tenant experience of eviction and re-colonisation on the earl of Clanricarde's lands in 19th-century Galway and the colonization of Ráth Cairn with Irish speakers in the 20th century. These local experiences cannot be a simple chronicling of events relating to an area within administrative or geographically determined boundaries since understanding a local world presents much more complex challenges for the historian. It is a reconstruction of the socially diverse worlds of the poor as well as the rich and a consideration of those who took widely contrasting positions on the political issues that preoccupied local communities in Ireland. Reconstructing such diverse local worlds relies on understanding what the people of the different communities that made up the localities of Ireland had in common and what drove them apart. Understanding the assumptions, often unspoken, around which these local societies operated is the key to recreating the world of the Irish past and reconstructing the way in which those who inhabited those worlds lived their daily lives. In addressing these issues, studies such as those presented in these short books, together with their predecessors, are at the forefront of Irish historical research and represent some of the most innovative and exciting work being undertaken in Irish history today. They also provide models which others can follow up and adapt in their own studies of the Irish past. In such ways will we understand better the regional diversity of Ireland and the social and cultural basis for that diversity. If they also convey something of the vibrancy and excitement of the world of Irish local history today they will have achieved at least some of their purpose.

Maynooth Studies in Local History: Number 98

Music and dancing at Castletown, County Kildare, 1759–1821

Karol Mullaney-Dignam

FOUR COURTS PRESS

Set in 10pt on 12pt Bembo by
Carrigboy Typesetting Services for
FOUR COURTS PRESS LTD
7 Malpas Street, Dublin 8, Ireland
www.fourcourtspress.ie
and in North America for
FOUR COURTS PRESS
c/o ISBS, 920 N.E. 58th Avenue, Suite 300, Portland, OR 97213.

ISBN 978–1–84682–296–4

Printed in England
by Antony Rowe Ltd, Chippenham, Wilts.

Contents

Acknowledgments   6

Introduction   7

1   Music and dancing in the social milieu of the Conollys   14

2   Occasions for music and dancing at Castletown   28

3   Masters, musicians, and music tradesmen   43

Conclusion   56

Notes   57

Acknowledgments

Sincere thanks are due to Professor Raymond Gillespie for accepting my contribution to this series and for his patience with my endeavour. I am also indebted to Dr Terence Dooley, Director of the Centre for the Study of Historic Irish Houses and Estates, Department of History, NUI Maynooth, for the opportunity to instigate there the 'Music in the Irish Country House' research project. This is the first significant resultant study, the initial research for which was supported by the Office of Public Works. A particular word of gratitude is owed to Ms Mary Heffernan whose comprehension of the relevance and potential of the project was crucial in its advancement. In 2010, I was awarded a two-year Irish Research Council for the Humanities and Social Sciences (IRCHSS) Government of Ireland Postdoctoral Fellowship to develop the project at NUI Maynooth. This IRCHSS funding of my research has been significant in ensuring the appropriate development and application of initial findings. In this regard, my mentors, Dr Terence Dooley and Professor Fiona Palmer, Head of the Department of Music, NUI Maynooth, have provided invaluable advice and assistance. Professors R.V. Comerford, Barra Boydell and Harry White have also been constant sources of encouragement. This particular study was enabled by a variety of people including friends and colleagues who provided helpful references to relevant sources. I am also grateful to the Castletown Foundation and the staff of the Office of Public Works at Castletown as well as the John Paul II Library and Russell Library at NUI Maynooth, National Library of Ireland, Irish Architectural Archive, Public Record Office of Northern Ireland, Irish Traditional Music Archive and Trinity College Dublin. A special word of thanks must go to Mr Finian Corley for his kindness and generosity in allowing me to examine the 'Castletown' manuscript music book in his possession. Mar fhocal scoir, ba mhaith liom mo bhuíochas ó chroí a ghabháil le mo thuismitheoirí, le mo dheirfiúracha agus le Pádraig as ucht a dtacaíocht leanúnach.

Introduction

The Castletown estate, adjoining the village of Celbridge in Co. Kildare, was acquired in the early 18th century by William Conolly (1662–1729) of Co. Donegal.[1] Although his origins are obscure William appears to have qualified as an attorney in Dublin in 1685. From the 1690s, he held a variety of employments, including that of legal agent to Captain James Hamilton (c.1661–1734), later 6th earl of Abercorn. As well as earning a considerable income from this agency work William made his fortune from dealing in large forfeited Jacobite estates. In 1709, he purchased the Castletown estate, from Thomas Dongan (1634–1715), 2nd earl of Limerick. William also had a very successful political career with the purchase of lands in the north of Ireland providing an electoral base. As an MP in the Irish house of commons, he represented Donegal in the 1690s and Co. Londonderry from 1703 to his death. In 1715, he rose to the highest political office in the state, that of Speaker of the Irish house of commons, a position he held until 1728. Thus, from the very outset, visitors to the existing house at Castletown included political allies.[2] Social connections had been brought about by his marriage, in 1694, to Katherine Conyngham (c.1662–1752) of Mount Charles, Co. Donegal.

William Conolly's success in business, politics and society was manifested in the great mansion, which he had begun on his Castletown estate around 1722. He was, by this time, one of the wealthiest landowners in Ireland with an annual rental income of around £17,000.[3] His new house, also known as Castletown, was the first of its kind in the country, built on a grand scale in the Palladian style, with a principal centre mansion flanked by colonnades leading to two service wings. Plans for the house had been drawn c. 1718 by the Italian architect Alessandro Galilei (1691–1737) but the interior scheme seems to have been the work of the Irish architect Edward Lovett Pearce (c.1699–1733). The actual building of Castletown was a collaborative effort supervised by Conolly himself over a number of years.[4]

Entertainment was clearly the function of the new house at Castletown, particularly of political allies, and visits there became customary for successive lords lieutenant or viceroys in Ireland. Some, like Charles FitzRoy (1683–1757), the 2nd duke of Grafton, retreated there from Dublin Castle in times of political crisis or when simply in need of a rest. After the Williamite wars, domiciliary entertaining, or the hosting of social gatherings such as assemblies, balls and dinner-parties in the home, was the primary form of sociability for the nobility and landed gentry in Ireland.[5] While social connections tended to provide political influence, political influence could, in turn, stem from the social cachet gained by the provision of good hospitality and entertainments. These aspects of social life, usually overseen by the women of the house, complemented and assisted the political or business interests of their husbands. This generally implied that the more influential the male head of household, the greater the social responsibility of his female counterpart.[6] Thus, the provision of hospitality and entertainments, as well as the decoration and furnishing of domiciliary spaces, were something more significant than mere female preoccupation.[7] Although there is a dearth of evidence, there is no reason to believe that music and dancing did not feature as part of the hospitality and entertainments on offer at Castletown in the time of William and Katherine Conolly. These were important aspects of the social life generally enjoyed by the Irish landed gentry in the early 18th century.

Most non-domiciliary occasions for music and dancing, in Dublin and in the provincial towns, reflected those of elite London society and were usually motivated by other aspects of life such as philanthropy and sociability. By the 1730s, the most distinctive feature of Irish musical life was the promotion of major choral works, such as oratorios, odes and anthems, for charitable purposes, including the support of hospitals and the relief of families of prisoners. Charitable institutions showed considerable fundraising ingenuity at this time and Mercer's Hospital, founded in 1734, was among the first to promote musical performances. It was in aid of this hospital that one of the most celebrated musical events in Irish history occurred in April 1742: the first performance of 'Messiah', directed by its composer George Frederick Handel (1685–1759). This premiere was the culmination of two series of subscription concerts which had begun in December 1741. Concert-going, however, was a social duty rather than a display of enthusiasm for music; it was usual for patrons to chat or play cards during performances.[8]

Katherine Conolly was typical of wealthy female philanthropists who urged acquaintances to purchase tickets for such non-domiciliary entertainments.[9] William had died in 1729, and despite the great house being unfinished and unfurnished, Katherine lived there for more than twenty years. During her widowhood, she gained renown as an arbiter of society and Castletown, located only 12 miles (*c.*20 kilometres) from Dublin, became a significant centre of hospitality, entertainment, and sociability. Toby Barnard has outlined how she established Castletown, initially as a rival social venue to Dublin Castle during the viceroyalty of the Lionel Sackville (1688–1765), the 1st duke of Dorset, in the early 1730s. Later it served as a complementary country base, to which William Cavendish (1698–1755), the 3rd duke of Devonshire, retreated from Dublin Castle in the late 1730s.[10]

The vice-regal court at Dublin Castle was at the centre of formal sociability in Ireland. The social dance occasions, or balls, held there were invitation-only events to which hundreds of the nobility and gentry were summoned.[11] Dancing at this level of society had lost much of the spontaneity and freedom of movement still present among the lower orders. The French court had led the way in this regard, fashioning 'peasant' or 'folk' dances into stylized exhibitions of contemporary courtesies, costumes and 'charm'. Participation in a ball, then, centred on performance rather than recreation, and dancing, being an important measure of breeding and grace, was the most admired type of performance. A dance known as the minuet epitomized the exhibitionist aspect of social dancing in the Georgian period. A slow, graceful, yet intricate, partner-dance, adapted by the French court around 1650, the minuet gained in such popularity that it had become the opening dance of almost every court ball and formal assembly in Europe by 1800.[12] It required years of practice to master the precise steps and constrained body movements and was, thus, more of a display of acquired social behaviour and deportment.[13] Exhibition dances like the minuet were performed as the opening dances at formal social occasions in Dublin Castle, particularly in vice-regal company, right into the 19th century. Dancing, then, was a proactive form of ritualized social interaction for the nobility and gentry. It was such a popular aspect of sociability that balls were held in a domiciliary context, in both the town and country house. Consequently, many occasions for music in the Irish country house were connected with social dancing.

The extent to which music and dancing featured as part of the hospitality provided at Castletown in the widowhood of Katherine Conolly is unknown. Her hospitality centred on managing the legacy of her late husband and advancing the political career of his nephew and heir, William James Conolly (1706–54). As the new head of the Conolly family and the man to whom Castletown was to devolve once her own life interest ceased, Katherine was anxious that he build on the reputation and achievements of his uncle. William was well-married to Lady Anne Wentworth (1713–97), a daughter of the diplomat earl of Strafford, Thomas Wentworth (1672–1739). He preferred horse-breeding and racing to politics and, being evidently less ambitious than his aunt, failed to secure any significant appointments. After Katherine's death in 1752, he moved his family into Castletown but died two years later. His only surviving son, Thomas, was still a minor and would not claim his inheritance for another four years. In the meantime, Castletown was lent as a country retreat to the new lord lieutenant, William Cavendish (1720–64), the marquis of Hartington, afterwards the 4th duke of Devonshire.[14]

The centrality of Castletown in Irish political and social life was, then, well-established by 1758 and the coming-of-age of Thomas Conolly (1738–1803). Thomas was educated at the Westminster School in London between 1750 and 1754 and, in 1755, at the Académie de Genève in Switzerland. He subsequently embarked upon his Grand Tour and was in Rome by 1758. The

Grand Tour was an essential rite of passage for young men of title or vast wealth, its primary value lying in the social and cultural edification it offered. While viewing sites and objects of classical antiquity, Renaissance works of arts and buildings of architectural significance, Thomas would also have been exposed to the fashionable dancing and modish music of the primary European cities in the mid-18th century. On his return from the Continent, Thomas went to his Castletown estate, where he met his young neighbour Louisa Lennox.

Lady Louisa Augusta Lennox (1743–1821) was the third surviving daughter of Lady Sarah Cadogan (1705–51) and her husband General Charles Lennox (1701–50), the 2nd duke of Richmond. The duke and duchess, whose country seat was at Goodwood near Chichester in the south-east of England, were both attached to the court of George II (1683–1760). They also had familial ties with the royal household, Richmond being the grandson of Charles II of England and his French mistress Louise de Kérouaille. Richmond had a keen interest in music; in 1725 he was elected as a governor of the Royal Academy of Music founded in the early 18th century to promote Italian opera in London. He was kept informed of the latest Italian productions through his correspondence with Owen MacSwiney (1675–1754), an Irish impresario based in Venice.[15] After the successive deaths of Richmond and his wife, the youngest Lennox children, Louisa, Sarah and Cecilia, were sent to Ireland to live with their elder sister Emily (1731–1814). Emily, a god-daughter of George II, lived at Carton, Co. Kildare, with her husband James FitzGerald (1722–73), then earl of Kildare.

Ladies of the nobility and landed gentry, like the Lennox sisters, were formally presented to society before they were 18 years of age and were precluded from attending formal non-domiciliary assemblies until they had made their 'debut'. The purpose of the debut was, largely, to display the debutante to the families of eligible bachelors. Elite Irish ladies were presented both at the vice-regal court at Dublin Castle and at court in London. In both cases, these presentations were made by application only and were bound by exacting etiquette. The debutante was summoned to attend her presentation on a particular day in full court attire and chaperoned by a lady of high social rank who had herself been previously presented. Thus, in 1758, a 14-year-old Louisa Lennox was presented in Dublin by her sister Emily, the countess of Kildare.[16] Presentations were usually followed by a ball where the debutante was expected to perform a minuet before the assembled company. Louisa had to have received appropriate instruction from a dancing-master in order to accomplish this.

The presentation of debutantes also marked the start of the Season, a hectic period of social activity which attended the annual exodus of landowning families from their country houses to the city and was coincident with the sitting of parliament. The purpose of the Season was for the landed gentry to meet peers in the wider social circle, to make political and business deals and to find suitable marriage partners for their children. In Dublin, the Season was also coincident with the arrival from England of the vice-regal representative, or lord lieutenant, and his wife at the vice-regal apartments at the Castle. There they formally lived 'in state' for a number of months and hosted a series of levees and drawing-rooms (formal receptions given in the morning or early afternoon) as well as banquets and balls (formal entertainments given in the evening).

Although Season events often began around Christmas-time and continued through to August, the Dublin Season peaked around St Patrick's Day (17 March) while the London Season got into full swing between Easter and July. A young lady, once presented, was considered eligible for marriage and attended as many of the balls, concerts, dances, breakfasts, dinner-parties, masquerades, soirées, military reviews and sporting events as possible, to ensure that she met worthy suitors. Most girls hoped to be engaged to be married within their first Season, and certainly by their third. Louisa was, by all accounts, possessed of the beauty peculiar to all of the Lennox sisters and had an abundance of admirers in her first Dublin Season. Among them was Garrett Wesley (1735–81), afterwards the 1st earl of Mornington, whose Irish estate was at Dangan in Co. Meath. Wesley was a politician who later fathered several distinguished British military commanders and politicians, including Arthur Wellesley (1769–1852), the 1st duke of Wellington. Wesley was also a prominent musician and composer educated at Trinity College Dublin in the early 1750s. As a composer he was known chiefly for his glees, most of which were published posthumously. He founded a prestigious academy of music in Dublin in 1757, which became well known for its charitable concerts. While professional (paid) performers, especially those attached to the theatres, were considered socially inferior it was acceptable in the 18th century for men of the nobility and landed gentry to practice as amateur (unpaid) musicians for charitable or entertaining purposes; Wesley epitomized the leadership of such amateur activity in Dublin at this time. He was elected the first professor of music in the University of Dublin in 1764.[17]

Had Louisa Lennox accepted Wesley's offer of marriage, she might have been enveloped more definitely in musical activity. However, she accepted the proposal of Thomas Conolly and they married on 30 December 1758. Thomas and Louisa are the first of the Conolly family about whom significant evidence of their social lives, and of the entertainments that they provided at Castletown, can still be found today. Music and dancing were integral to those entertainments. Direct evidence of this has been gleaned for this study from a variety of primary source materials currently available across a number of repositories in Ireland and the United Kingdom including: personal and household account books, tradesmen's receipt books and the voluminous correspondences of the Lennox sisters.[18]

It appears from these sources that many of the Conollys' first social experiences together were in London and Dublin, rather than at Castletown. This is not surprising for three reasons; first, given the fact that they both had strong family ties in England which they maintained right throughout their lives. Second, the Conollys were expected to spend time in London because Thomas was involved in political affairs, having been elected to the English house of commons in 1759. He continued to officially reside in Ireland, though, and was elected in 1761 to the Irish house of commons as an MP for Co. Londonderry. In the same year, he was also appointed to the Privy Council of Ireland, acquiring the right to style himself as 'the Right Honourable Thomas Conolly'. Third, despite the fact that Castletown had been a centre of hospitality and entertainment in the time of Katherine Conolly, parts of the house were not yet completed. There was no grand staircase and many of the rooms were unfinished, unfurnished or now unfashionable. Thomas and Louisa undertook an extensive project of remodelling and decoration which occupied them for much of the 1760s and early 1770s. Although there is evidence that some music and dancing occurred at Castletown during these years, large-scale entertainments would have been hindered by the ongoing improvements to the house.

By its very nature, domiciliary sociability attracted less contemporary attention than more public forms of sociability at the theatres or the vice-regal court. Notices and reports concerning entertainments in the domestic sphere were not generally found in the newspapers of the day. Thus, it is easy for the historian to overlook or understate the extent and significance of aspects of domiciliary entertainments such as music and dancing. This is reflected, to a large degree, in the historiography surrounding Castletown where specialist studies have, for many reasons, tended to focus on aspects of architecture, material culture and landscape as well as family histories and biographies.[19] While these studies are indispensable, particularly with regard to understanding the material expressions of the nobility and landed gentry in the 18th and 19th centuries, domiciliary sociability remains a neglected research topic. This is notwithstanding the fact that a scholarly examination of domiciliary entertainment, in particular, would provide new perspectives on the form, function and furnishing of Irish country houses in general. This particular study of music and dancing at Castletown in the period from 1759 to 1821, hopes to demonstrate the significance of scholarship in this direction.

In order to appreciate the nature and function of music and dancing at Castletown, it is first necessary to understand the place of these activities in the Conollys' broader social milieu, particularly in the 1760s and early 1770s. This is the focus of the first chapter of this study, which contextualizes the occasions for music and dancing which occurred at Castletown in the 1770s and 1780s. These years marked a zenith of music and dancing as aspects of domiciliary sociability at Castletown and coincided with the period during which the Conollys were more invested than ever in Irish society and in domestic life. Around the same time we find music and dancing functioning at Castletown in the contexts of education and employment. Thus, the third chapter of this study considers those who facilitated music and dancing at Castletown and in the social lives of the extended Conolly family from the 1780s into the early 19th century.

1. Music and dancing in the social milieu of the Conollys

Thomas and Louisa Conolly's first social experiences as a newly-married society couple were in England, to where they travelled, on the vice-regal yacht, in March 1759. Their arrival was marked by a ball given by Louisa's brother Charles Lennox (1735–1806), the 3rd duke of Richmond, at which Louisa was reported to have behaved most appropriately and danced 'charmingly'.[1] She was also presented at court by her eldest sister Lady Caroline Fox (1723–74). There she met King George II and the king's grandson and successor, Prince George of Wales (1738–1820). From April 1759, the Conollys took a house at Grosvenor Square in London. From there, Thomas attended to his parliamentary business while Louisa made her debut on the London Season, which was then in full swing. Louisa did not have the pressure of securing a marriage partner and so enjoyed the activity that attended the Season. Non-domiciliary entertainments included operas, plays and a ridotto. The latter usually consisted of a concert followed by dancing, in which the audience joined with the performers, something which Louisa liked best 'of all things'.[2]

Being connected to the elite of London society, the Conollys also received invitations to the most exclusive social events held at the town houses of the leading members of the nobility. They attended a 'vastly pleasant' ball, given by the duke and duchess of Bedford at Bedford House, for example, where they met other members of the royal family. Louisa danced with a number of men including her Irish neighbour, Edward Wingfield (1729–64), the 2nd Viscount Powerscourt. She also saw the famously beautiful Maria Gunning (c.1732–60), then countess of Coventry, dancing a minuet 'charmingly'.[3] So hectic was their combined social itinerary that Louisa's brother-in-law, the earl of Kildare, reported to his wife: 'I never see the Conollys; they are running about everywhere like mad people'.[4] When not in the company of her husband, Louisa was accompanied at social events by family members, including her mother-in-law, Lady Anne Conolly.

The time soon came for the Conollys to host a ball of their own and so their first such experience was not at Castletown but at their rented house in London. Their ball, held on 26 April 1759, was, by all accounts, a significant affair attended by members of the extended Lennox family, society beauties, members of the royal family, including Prince Edward Augustus (1739–67), and a number of Irish neighbours. Although the ball received general approval, the politician and writer Horace Walpole (1717–97) felt that 'the ball at Mr Conolly's was by no means delightful; the house is small, it was hot and composed of young Irish'.[5] Louisa, however, was delighted with her first hosting experience. While acknowledging that there were 'too many people', she told her sister Emily: 'I am glad our ball was approved of. I danced with Lord Powerscourt, Prince Edward and a few more that I don't recollect'.[6]

It is not known who supplied the music for the Conollys' ball but, considering the company, formal exhibition dances like the minuet undoubtedly featured. Thus, the ball would have opened around 8 p.m. with a minuet performed by the male and female of highest distinction present, followed in order of social rank by other couples. The minuets would have lasted for anything up to two hours, after which other forms of dancing commenced. After about an hour of these dances, there would have been an interval for supper. The provision of refreshments was a fundamental feature of every type of entertainment and at a ball these were usually served in a room separate to the ball-room. While dancing would have recommenced around midnight, dining probably occurred in tandem with the dancing owing to the numbers of people involved. Those highest in rank danced first and dined first; Prince Edward dined with Louisa at her table. In another room, five card tables were set up for those not wishing to dance to play games of loo, quadrille and cribbage. Gambling on card-games was an integral aspect of sociability at this time and featured at domiciliary and non-domiciliary entertainments. Not only was it typical in the late 18th century for gambling to occur at a fashionable ball but also for dancing to continue into the early hours of the following morning – the moral hazards of such activity were the subject of the occasional published treatise.[7]

From June to August 1759, the Conollys moved to Stretton Hall, the family's house in Staffordshire, where Louisa happily took part in all of the available country diversions. Caroline Fox was pleased to report to the countess of Kildare that their sister was 'as happy dancing country dances with his [Mr Conolly's] sisters, one or two other people he has in the house, and the servants, as at the finest ball in town'.[8] Country dances were the dances most likely to be performed in an informal context and were also performed after the minuets at court balls, including those held at Dublin Castle. They had developed from formalized versions of 'folk' or 'country' dances and were popularized by their inclusion in numerous dance manuals published in the late 17th century.[9] Most of these dances would have originally taken place outdoors 'for as many as will' in a variety of formations including 'square', 'round' and 'long'. The formalization and refinement of such dances by the 18th century meant that dancing in large square, circle (round) or line (long) configurations was reduced for indoor practice, mainly to square arrangements for four, six or eight people.[10] While there would have been some cross-over, it seems that there were distinctions between country dances of a stylized and fashionable nature performed by the nobility and gentry and those of a more traditional nature performed by their servants and tenants. Many of the country dances published in Ireland in the 18th century were actually newly-invented indoor dances in a country-dance style as opposed to being 'country' in the sense of tradition or authenticity.[11] Some of these dances would have been performed to well-known tunes suitable for dancing while others would have been performed to newly composed music.

Nonetheless, many of the 'longways as many as will' configurations resembled the rincí fada (long dances) danced outdoors by the Irish tenantry to jig music.[12] Compact indoor versions of long dances were performed where space allowed in the Irish and in the English country house. They generally featured two rows of dancers, one line of men facing one line of women, the left hand-side of the men and the right-hand side of the women being to the top of the room. The leading couple at the top of the row chose the dance and performed the figures down the row until they reached the second couple. The second couple then began to dance, imitating the figures done by the first couple. Gradually the first couple danced down to the bottom of the row, each couple imitating the first in a sort of domino effect, until all couples were moving.[13]

After spending the summer country-dancing at Stretton Hall, the Conollys returned to Ireland in October 1759. There, while Thomas attended to parliamentary business and sporting pursuits, Louisa occupied herself with planning the refurbishment of Castletown and maintaining a correspondence with her younger sister Sarah (1745–1826). Sarah was now living in London where, much to the excitement of the family, she was being courted by the new king, George III.[14] Louisa's letters to her over the years provide much of the information that we have today about the Conollys' social milieu in Ireland. Domiciliary entertainment was, evidently, the primary form of sociability for the Irish nobility and landed gentry at this time. During the Dublin Season this tended to be centred on the town house but it also occurred in country houses relatively close to Dublin.

In the town or the country, management of the household, being the female domain, usually conferred hosting responsibilities upon the female head of the family. Hence, we find Louisa attending a flurry of events hosted by women in 1760, including a ball by Lady Louth where she only danced 'ten dances the whole night and all of them with old men'.[15] Unmarried men, young and old, also hosted entertainments although it was usually the responsibility of a reliable female friend to issue invitations and to organize the requisite food, decoration and entertainments. Sometimes women borrowed the homes of their male friends to host entertainments of their own. Hence, in December

1760, we find Louisa preparing for hosting duties at the home of Lord Powerscourt, who had 'been so good as to promise me a ball. We have fixed it for next Friday'. Even though she did not describe the details of the event to her sister, she did reveal afterwards that it was 'the most delightful, agreeable, pleasant ball that ever was'.[16] In the same month, Louisa attended a ball hosted in Dublin by Francis Thomas FitzMaurice (1740–1818), the 3rd earl of Kerry, a lengthy description of which was provided to Sarah. This account, occasioned by her annoyance at a man named 'Dilan or Diland', is interesting for what it reveals about the conventions of dancing at a ball. Louisa wrote that she had agreed to dance two dances with this man, after which he asked her to dance on for the next two with him. However, this was 'a thing one never does but with the most agreeable partners. I told him that was not the custom'. She was then forced to sit out the rest of the dancing because he could not find another partner and told her that if she were to dance any more he wished it to be with him: 'As I would not I thought it would be rude to dance with anybody else and, therefore, was obliged to sit down which I did not much like and, therefore, I had the mortification of going home at five o'clock, it being so early to leave the ball.'[17]

Louisa also went to formal balls at Dublin Castle but she found these far less enjoyable than domiciliary balls, even if they did afford her an appropriate opportunity to wear her new 'diamond cap' in April 1761. By this time, however, the endless round of social activity was already beginning to take its toll on her as she declared to Sarah: 'I am grown a great gambler and am very fond of pharo, I don't love dancing so passionately as I used to do, and I am grown very thin'.[18] The following Season she attended but a few balls at the Castle, even though the viceroyalty of George Montagu-Dunk (1716–71), the 2nd earl of Halifax, brought with it a busy round of entertainments. She opted instead to participate in domiciliary activities, these being 'the pleasantest'. But, as she told Sarah, there were 'not so many private balls as there used to be'.[19] Although many domiciliary activities were often contemporaneously described as 'private', this was actually where the majority of social interaction occurred among the nobility and landed gentry.[20] The lack of such sociability around Dublin in December 1762 was a source of complaint for Louisa: 'we are invited to a ball at Lord Kerry's … He is the only body that thinks of diverting the town; everybody else is mightily stupid.'[21]

Dublin was still 'more stupid than anything ever was' in 1767 but formal society went on at the Castle, now under the administration of Viscount George Townshend (1724–1807), who would be lord lieutenant until 1772.[22] His role was now more proactive, particularly with regard to parliamentary management, and becoming acquainted with the Irish landowning and governing elite was more important than ever. Lady Charlotte Townshend had a vastly significant position as an animator and arbiter of fashionable society but she relied on prominent society women, like Louisa Conolly, to make introductions. Hence, in 1768, we find Louisa going to Dublin more than ever 'to wait upon Lady Townshend' when she 'saw company'.[23]

The lord lieutenant was now also required to become permanently resident in Ireland; previously, he and his wife only temporarily resided in Dublin during the Season.[24] This requirement exposed the unsuitability of the vice-regal apartments at Dublin Castle as a full-time family residence. Over the years a number of alternative residences would be used but that favoured by the Townshend household was Leixlip Castle in Co. Kildare, a property owned by the Conolly family. Speaker William Conolly had purchased the castle in 1728 and it had passed as part of the Conolly inheritance to Thomas 30 years later. It had been let to various friends of the Conollys over the years, including the archbishop of Armagh, George Stone (1708–64). Thomas and Louisa had themselves stayed there when Castletown was temporarily uninhabitable in 1765.[25] The Townshends were settled in Leixlip Castle by June 1768 from where they regularly visited the Conollys. Entertaining the vice-regal household and waiting on Lady Townshend at the vice-regal court were viewed by Louisa as responsibilities of her 'rank and station in life'.[26]

Another responsibility entrusted to her by her sister Emily, now the duchess of Leinster, who had given birth to 15 children by 1768, was the chaperoning of female family members to various entertainments. In the first years of their marriage the Conollys spent a large portion of their time with the FitzGeralds, both at Carton in Co. Kildare and at Leinster (previously Kildare) House in Dublin. In the Season of 1768, Louisa accompanied her younger sister Lady Cecilia Lennox (1750–69) and her niece Lady Emily FitzGerald (1752–1818) to a number of balls in Dublin. She considered as particularly pleasant a ball given by the Conollys' friend Robert Sandford (*c.*1722–93). It being the fashion of the time, Cecilia and Emily were 'powdered' for the occasion. Powdering was a cosmetic camouflaging of the hair in grey powder, the natural hair being enhanced with horse-hair pieces and combed-up extensions which did not necessarily match the natural hair-colour. Louisa told her sister Sarah that while her powdered charges danced until four o'clock in the morning, she only danced a little 'just by way of not giving up dancing because sometimes I may have a fancy to dance, and when once one has quite left off one is ashamed to begin again. I, therefore, do generally dance one or two dances, though I don't love it'.[27]

February 1768 was a hectic month and Louisa was also involved in preparations for a lavish ball at the Castle. Both she and her charges, Cecilia and Emily, wore gowns 'of Irish manufacture' because Louisa considered herself to be 'a great patriot'. Although the Castle 'was extremely full' and very hot, Louisa commented that both girls danced very well. 'Poor Emily', however, 'was in such a fright that she trembled from head to foot. And though she might have danced better if she had not been frightened, yet her fright was no disadvantage to her for she looked so modest and gentle that it was impossible not to admire her'.[28] Evidently, Emily's restrained body movements, occasioned by her nerves, ensured an appropriately refined exhibition of modesty and charm. Louisa was very proud of the fact that Cecilia and Emily were much admired as it reflected on her as their chaperone and mentor.[29]

While she always obliged in her social responsibilities, Louisa still did not enjoy being in Dublin. In May 1768, for example, she wrote: 'I hear there is to be a ball for the king's birthday but I hope Cecilia and Emily won't want me to go, for such a crowd in summer is very disagreeable.' She much preferred being at her house at Castletown, where refurbishment works were slowly progressing. She confided to Sarah: 'I long to be settled there'.[30] Thomas was of similar mind and opted to spend as little time in the city as possible. Like his father, he was keen on breeding and racing horses and regularly raced a number of his own at the Curragh race-course in Co. Kildare.[31] The races were attended by music and dancing and usually culminated in a ball at the nearby assembly rooms.

Assembly rooms were to be found in most Irish cities, towns and social centres by the end of the 18th century.[32] They were sometimes connected with a prominent building, such as the town hall, and were capable of facilitating hundreds of people. They usually comprised a set of rooms with different social functions, including dancing, dining, card-playing and tea-drinking. While some assemblies occurred without dancing or music, the focus being on gossiping and flirtation over the card-tables, promoters generally ensured that a range of entertainments, from concerts of vocal and instrumental music to lavish balls, were provided. The large and sumptuous spaces provided by assembly rooms also allowed for the popularization of varieties of country-dancing, including the 'longways progressive, for as many as will' configuration.[33]

The popularity of assembly rooms probably accounted for the occasional ebb in domiciliary entertainments of which Louisa complained to her sister. The nobility and gentry, who patronized these venues, usually did so by paying an advance subscription, in return for which they received a ticket. This transferable subscription ticket permitted entry to all entertainments which occurred there within a certain period. Admission was also available to approved persons on the night of a particular entertainment, but at a higher cost. Tickets for ladies usually cost less than those for gentlemen and were available from members of a subscription committee, some of whom were leading patrons. Being a leading society lady, Louisa Conolly was a patroness for various subscription balls held at the Rotunda assembly rooms in Dublin from the late 1760s.

The Rotunda was a large circular assembly venue attached to the Lying-in Hospital in Dublin. While the maternity hospital had been founded in 1745, the Rotunda was added in 1767 to provide for fund-raising entertainments and so became one of the most significant locations for musical activity in Ireland in the late 18th century.[34] It, as well the pleasure gardens and bowling-green at the rear of the hospital, were opened on summer evenings for 'excellent concerts of vocal and instrumental music'. Sunday evening concerts were vastly popular and were a weekly 'brilliant assembly of the first people in Dublin'. Most of the expenses of the hospital were defrayed by the receipts of these summer concerts as well as the proceeds of subscription balls held at the Rotunda in the winter months.[35]

It was with these fund-raising balls that Louisa Conolly was primarily associated. The duke of Leinster was on the board of hospital governors and, along with the duchess of Leinster, Louisa was one of the chief lady-patronesses. Their names, along with those of other patronesses such as the countesses of Charlemont, Belvedere, Ely, and Rosse, were printed in newspaper advertisements to attract company of quality. The selectness of the assembly was preserved, and noted in a designated subscription book, by these patronesses as tickets were only available by application to them.[36] The tickets for men were black in colour and usually cost one guinea (£1 1s.) while those for women were usually half a guinea (10s. 6d.) and red in colour.

Although the music for the Rotunda balls was rarely advertised, it usually comprised a small band of musicians playing music suitable for dancing. It also appears that many balls were attended in, what Louisa called, 'habit' or fancy-dress. A habit ball was not, as she pointed out to Sarah, to be confused with 'a masquerade, for it is not one and people think that you mean to laugh at them by calling it a masquerade where there are no masks'.[37] Masquerade had been introduced in London in the early 1700s and involved the adoption of a fancy-dress disguise and masks while partaking in the usual activities associated with a ball. Even when there were no masks, fancy-dress balls were invariably referred to as masquerades.

The dominance of domiciliary entertainments, and their impact on non-domiciliary assemblies and fundraising activities, is highlighted by the concluding line in an advertisement for the 1777 annual Rotunda ball which expressed the hope 'that none of the nobility or gentry will injure the charity by any private ball'.[38] The assembly room, however, was also having a reciprocal impact upon domiciliary sociability. Ambitious families, such as the Conollys, were modifying their country houses in order to emulate assembly room sociability, particularly in terms of the overall scale and the simultaneity of activities.[39]

At a time when most entertaining was done at home, assembly rooms were one of the two primary non-domiciliary venues of entertainment, open to both sexes. The other was the playhouse, or theatre, and although she did not like being in Dublin, Louisa did enjoy going to see plays when she was there.

Music and dancing had long been aspects of theatre-going in Dublin, music usually featuring in interludes between the acts of spoken plays or in light-hearted after-pieces. The theatre at Smock Alley was opened in 1662 as the first custom-built playhouse in Dublin and became the first theatre outside of London to receive a royal patent. Regarded as the finest playhouse in Dublin, it attracted the greatest stage-actors of the time. These included the Dublin-born Spranger Barry (1717–77) who made his debut there in 1744 and had many successful years on the stage in London.

There were intense rivalries among playhouses, actors and audiences in late 18th-century Dublin and, in 1758, Barry opened a playhouse on Crow Street to rival Smock Alley. The patronage of the nobility and landed gentry was vital for the success of any playhouse, as the audience was on display as much as the players on stage. While audiences were, to an extent, socially diverse, the arrangement of the auditorium and the admission prices ensured social segregation. The seating was usually designed in a horse-shoe shape around the stage which was fully illuminated by candles. In the 'pit' or flat area, below or at the same level as the stage, people sat for a price of 3s. 3d. on cloth-covered benches. Above them, towards the rear of the auditorium, were two or three stories of galleries of seats where those of the highest social status sat lowest down and those of the lower social status sat higher. A seat in the lower gallery usually cost around 4s. 4d. and one in the upper gallery around 1s. 6d.[40]

The galleries were usually noisy and sometimes even riotous. In order to encourage more quality clientele Barry offered highly ambitious and elaborately staged productions, and insisted that strict etiquette be observed, at his Crow Street theatre. Quality patrons also required exclusive seating, an important source of additional revenue. The boxes, typically placed immediately to the front and side above the level of the stage, contained the most prestigious seats in the house. They were usually separate rooms, with an open viewing area which sat about five people. Only the wealthy could afford to pay the 5s. 5d. admission price.

Spranger Barry was clearly successful in his efforts for, as early as February 1759, Louisa Conolly was spotted at Crow Street with her sisters Sarah and Emily.[41] In February 1762, she told Sarah that she was to bespeak, or sponsor, the performance of a play there.[42] She was there again in December of that year to see a performance of Nicholas Rowe's tragedy, *Jane Shore* (1714), which was followed by a farce called 'A trip to the Dargil'. Accompanied by her sisters Cecilia and Emily and some of the FitzGerald children, they all 'filled a row in the front box (for there we sat to see it in perfection) very prettily'.[43] In January 1767, Louisa reported to Sarah that the Crow Street playhouse was still 'in a good way and liked very much in general'.[44]

These theatres had resident orchestras and were central to the musical activity available in Dublin at this time. By the late 18th century, a tradition of ballad-opera had developed there alongside the promotion of major choral works for charitable purposes. Popularized by John Gay's *The beggar's opera*, first produced in London in January 1728, a ballad-opera usually comprised a comic plot-line into which a pastiche of songs, and sometimes instrumental interludes, were worked. The songs, which alternated with spoken dialogue, were usually set to well-known traditional ballad-tunes or contemporary popular melodies and were sung by the actors on stage.[45]

Although intended as a harsh and subtle satire on 'serious' Italianate opera, a hugely successful production of *The beggar's opera* at the Smock Alley theatre in March 1728 precipitated an enduring demand in Dublin for entertainments that combined drama with popular music, singing and even dancing. This was encouraged by the fact that only theatres licensed by royal patent, like Smock Alley, could put on serious spoken-only plays. Other theatres were only permitted to show novelty entertainments, circus acts and comedic drama interspersed with music, singing or dancing. Nevertheless, a spoken-only play was almost always followed by a farce or other novelty attraction featuring music and, sometimes, dancing. Some patrons attended for the farce only at a reduced cost of 2s. 6d.[46]

It seems that contemporary audiences did not necessarily expect or require clear distinctions between the various types of musical productions that they experienced. Louisa Conolly referred to any theatre she attended as 'the Play House', and her experiences there as 'the Play'. However, contemporary newspaper advertisements indicate that most of the plays seen by her would have included more or less in the way of music. Some were actually spoof-operas with satirical lyrics written to the tunes of popular songs of the day. Others were pantomimes or fast-paced farces with comedic plot-lines based on improbable scenarios, mistaken identity and sexual innuendo. Thus, it is difficult for the historian to distinguish between the varieties of musical comedy popular at this time and the plays that simply featured incidental music or interpolated songs.[47]

One form of musical entertainment that was contemporaneously distinct was opera. A serious art form that began in Italy in the 1500s, an opera was a dramatic work which combined text (libretto) with a musical score and was performed by professional singers and musicians. From the early 1760s, both the Crow Street and Smock Alley theatres had begun to present Italianate operas. However, as T.J. Walsh has shown, many of these operas tended to be of the *opéra bouffe*, or comic-opera, variety.[48] While most stage-actors were required to be able to sing, vocal specialists were required to perform operas and theatres were required to hire specialist opera companies from London and the Continent to produce quality performances. Hence, a night at the opera usually cost Louisa 10s. 6d., almost twice the price of any type of musical comedy or play featuring music.[49] This also meant that the evening's entertainment comprised only one type of production without the usual addition of a farce or other novelty attraction. Although Louisa's father, the 2nd duke of Richmond, had been a devotee of opera, she did not care much for it commenting, in 1771, that it was 'more tiresome' than attending a session in the Irish house of commons – something that she had also done.[50]

Despite her general enjoyment of theatre, Louisa still preferred to be away from the metropolis. In the summer of 1768, the Conollys purchased a house at the seaside resort of Blackrock, a small village about four miles south of the centre of the city overlooking Dublin bay. Many 'personages of the first distinction' had houses there, including the duke and duchess of Leinster.[51] They were located so close to the Conollys' lodge that, as Louisa told Sarah, it was like being in the same house. She enjoyed the company of the FitzGerald children but expressed the hope that other people would not 'plague' her 'with visiting'. At Blackrock, Louisa relaxed by bathing and engaging in self-improving activities such as learning to speak Italian (as she was already fluent in French) and learning to play the guitar. She told Sarah that she was a little anxious that she was 'too old' to learn guitar easily but felt that having a master 'come so far out of town' every morning was 'a good opportunity and good diversion'.[52] Although she did not reveal the name of her music-master to Sarah, an entry in Louisa's account book which reads 'paid Mr Claget [sic] for 15 lessons, a music book and strings £5 19s. 9d.', points to one of the two Claggett brothers resident in Dublin at this time.[53] The Claggets were prominent theatre musicians and composers, who appear to have both been born in Ireland but had early musical careers in Edinburgh, Scotland, where they published a set of violin duets and 40 *lessons and 12 songs for citra or guitar* around 1760. The elder Clagget, Charles (*c.*1740–*c.*1795), was a maker of musical instruments and novel musical devices. In the 1760s, he directed concerts at the Rotunda Gardens and led orchestras at the Smock Alley and Crow Street theatres in Dublin before his departure to London around 1770. Also employed in these orchestras was his brother, William (*c.*1741–*c.*1798).

Theatre orchestras offered the principal employment for professional musicians in Ireland and income was usually supplemented through music-teaching. As well as practical instruction, music-masters also provided requisite learning materials to their pupils. Mr Clagget, for example, supplied Louisa with a music book, presumably his own published volume of lessons and songs, as well as strings for her guitar. The instrument in question was a small, ten-stringed instrument held in the lap and commonly known today as the 'English' guitar. Being easy to learn, it was very much in vogue with elite ladies like Louisa. Her repertory was probably influenced by fashion, and by her teacher, and so would have consisted principally of solo arrangements of theatre songs and dance-tunes.[54] Louisa's verdict of her own guitar-playing was that she was making 'a most miserable progress, however it diverts me'.[55]

Diversion, and the maintenance of good spirits, seems to have been the purpose of musical instruction for young ladies in the 18th century.[56] One of the few things that affected Louisa Conolly's spirits was her 'nasty Northern journey'.[57] As Thomas was the sitting MP for Co. Londonderry, the Conollys were obliged to engage in social duties in that constituency, particularly prior to elections every seven years. According to Louisa, 'the duties attendant on an election' were 'assizes, races and balls'.[58] In 1768, Louisa complained to Sarah that they were 'obliged to go to some odious races in the North, the consequence of elections. Oh, how I do hate the very name of elections'.[59] She had considerably less difficulty, though, in going to England for the same purpose. By the 1770s, the Conollys had established a pattern of travelling to England during the first few months of the year where a number of weeks were spent with relatives. When in London Thomas involved himself in parliamentary and other business while Louisa participated in many of the same activities that occupied her in Dublin. She was fond of dinner parties and of playing cards to which she lost the hefty sum of £22 1s. in one night in March 1770. As well as doing the rounds of the grand town houses of the nobility and gentry, Louisa also attended events at more 'public' social venues such as Almack's.

Opened in 1765, Almack's was the most exclusive of London's assembly rooms. It had come to be governed by a small arbitration committee of the most influential ladies in London. Exclusivity was maintained by only allowing approved persons to purchase non-transferable admission tickets. Wealth did not guarantee admission; breeding and behaviour were considered more important. Louisa Conolly was undoubtedly pre-approved for entry and she attended a 'government' ball there on 9 February 1770. She had also received an invitation to a ball at the Mansion House on the same night but because her husband supported the government and that ball was to be attended by members of the opposition, she was obliged to decline the invitation. She considered as absurd the politicizing of a social event: 'To be sure it does seem odd that men should carry party as far as a ball. One has heard of women doing these sort of things, but, in either, I do think it is ridiculous.'[60] Almack's appears to have been opened to rival Mrs Teresa Cornely's establishment at Carlisle House in Soho Square, whose masquerade entertainments, though popular, had gained some notoriety by the 1770s.[61]

Nevertheless, Cornely's played host to one of the chief social events of the 1770 Season: a masquerade ball, held on Monday 27 February, attended by 800 of the principal nobility and gentry in London. At 9 p.m. the doors of the house were opened, and for three or four hours the company poured into the assembly. At mid-night the lower rooms of the house were opened for supper. According to a contemporary report, 'the richness and brilliancy of the dresses were almost beyond imagination; nor did any assembly ever exhibit a collection of more elegant and beautiful female figures'.[62] Among them was Louisa who stressed to her sister Emily that the event, organized and managed by 'sixteen gentlemen', was 'very proper'. She added: 'I was never more diverted than at the masquerade; it was one of the prettiest sights I ever saw. The house at Soho is well calculated for it, there were 800 people, but not the least crowd, scarcely too hot.' Having room enough to move around made the evening pleasant for Louisa as she could see everybody with ease. She was fascinated by the variety of ridiculous and pretty costumes on display, including men in the clothes of old women. Thomas Conolly dressed as 'a Spaniard' while Louisa dressed as an abbess with a 'white corded tabby, gauze and beads, a black veil and scarlet knot to tie the diamond cross'. She thought her outfit so plain that nobody would notice it yet Horace Walpole and others 'admired it vastly, and said it was very pretty'. It is not clear whether or not masks were actually worn at this masquerade; it appears that the aim for many of the ladies in attendance was to look as beautiful as possible in their fancy-dress. Those in 'eastern dresses', of Greece, India and China, were considered the finest. Although the company began to depart around 2 a.m., the Conollys stayed until the end of the festivities at 5 a.m.[63]

Despite the success of the 1770 masquerade attended by the Conollys, Cornely's appears to have gone bankrupt soon thereafter, the patronage of the nobility and gentry having transferred to the new assembly rooms at the Pantheon. Opened in 1772 and reminiscent of the Pantheon in Rome, it was one of the largest entertainment spaces in England, capable of facilitating over 1,500 people. The entertainments there included a variety of assemblies as well as masquerade balls and subscription concerts. Louisa patronized the Pantheon shortly after its opening, paying 5s. for a ticket on 24 April 1772. She also continued her patronage of Almack's where, in January 1773, she had been 'tempted' to go by her sister-in-law Caroline Hobart (c.1755–1817), the countess of Buckinghamshire. The crowd, though, was 'very thin, so much so, that the ladies were obliged to dance together'.[64]

Ranelagh Gardens in Chelsea was also one of Louisa's favourite non-domiciliary entertainment venues in London. These pleasure gardens, which had opened to the public in 1742, were an important venue for social dancing and musical concerts. She had been taken there from a relatively young age, when she and her sisters travelled from Ireland to visit relatives.[65] While 'public' pleasure gardens facilitated outdoor music and dancing they also usually contained indoor spaces for balls and musical concerts. They were more commercial establishments than assembly rooms and tended to have less exclusive rules on admission. Yet, they were frequented by the likes of Louisa Conolly and her friends.[66] In London, Louisa also experienced music in the patent theatres at Covent Garden and Drury Lane, and in the summer-theatre at Haymarket, where she sat in a box with family members or friends. She sometimes purchased a playbook or 'a pamphlet' for a price between 1s. and 2s. She saw many premiere productions and all of the great stage-actors of the time, including the highly influential David Garrick (1717–79). In March 1771, she went to the Theatre Royal at Covent Garden to see 'Clementina' a new production by Hugh Kelly (1739–77).[67] Kelly was an Irish journalist and dramatist whose plays, although controversial, were popular on the London stage during the 1770s. She also saw a musical production of 'Elfrida' at Covent Garden in January 1773. This was based on the tragic poem *Elfrida* (1752) by William Mason (1725–97) and was set to music by the composer Thomas Arne (1710–78), one of the most significant figures in 18th-century English theatre music.

By the late 1770s, Louisa was quite the theatre *connoisseur* and often met theatre personae like Garrick at domiciliary entertainments hosted by her friends. Although she found operas 'tiresome' she attended plenty of them in London. In 1773, she told Emily that she liked an opera she had just seen 'rather better than usual, as there was a good deal of chorus, which I like better than the fine songs [arias]'. There was also dancing by the ballerina Anne Heinel (1753–1808) which suggests that the entertainment in question was, perhaps, more of a ballet than an opera. Ballet, which had its origins in the social exhibitionist dancing of France and Italy, had developed into a professional art-form by the end of the 17th century but was danced on stage in regular clothing and shoes. Heinel was regarded as one of the foremost female dancers of the time and Louisa thought her 'charming; she does dance most delightfully and so much better than what there has been for some years'.[68]

The Conollys' sociability in England, and exposure to music and dancing, was not confined to London. They regularly visited relatives in Sussex and Staffordshire and partook in the entertainments on offer there. During the 1760s, they visited Bury St Edmunds in Suffolk, where Louisa's sister Sarah lived following her marriage, in 1762, to Charles Bunbury (1740–1821). Bury was a lively market town and the annual fair there culminated in a fine assembly to which Louisa Conolly purchased a ticket on 10 October 1766. Among the various purchases she made at the fair itself, was 'a music book' for which she paid 2s. 6d. In April 1771, she gave the same amount to bell-ringers at Bath, the fashionable spa resort in the south-west of England. Having some of the largest assembly rooms outside of London, it was ideal for large country-dance configurations. By the late 1760s, it was also a hub of musical entertainment where Louisa attended musical concerts for the usual box-fee of 5s.[69]

During her lifetime, Louisa also experienced music and dancing further afield. In 1765, for example, she spent three months in Paris with her sisters Sarah and Caroline, Caroline's sons and other friends.[70] As well attending social events in the city, Louisa's party was presented to the French king, Louis XV (1710–74), at his private residence, Château de Marly. They also visited Louis

Francois de Bourbon (1717–76), the prince of Conti, at his country château at L'Isle-Adam where they were treated to musical concerts of the *comédie-Italienne* variety every evening. Distinctions had been made in 17th-century Paris between so-called 'French' and 'Italian' entertainments, the former being considered the more serious and high-brow. However, Louisa and her contemporaries generally referred to serious music as 'Italian' and there was a proliferation of singers, instrumentalists and composers of that nationality in concert-life in Ireland and England.[71] Nevertheless, as in Dublin and London, *opéra bouffe* and comic musical plays were now so much the rage in Paris that the prince of Conti had his own music troupe of theatrical performers at L'Isle-Adam. Caroline considered this type of entertainment 'very pretty for those [who] love that light kind of music'.[72]

As well as returning to Paris, Louisa would travel to other European cities, including The Hague, in the later years of her life. The Lennox family had long-standing ties with The Hague; Louisa's mother, the 2nd duchess of Richmond, had been born there in 1705. By the mid-1770s, however, Louisa had grown somewhat tired of travelling and, particularly, of visiting London during the Season, calling it a 'vile town' in 1775.[73] From then on, the Conollys contrived to spend more time in Ireland and Louisa focused on her role in Dublin society. Besides, the refurbishment works were coming to an end at their home and Castletown was fast becoming a centre of sociability where music and dancing were the primary agents of entertainment.

2. Occasions for music and dancing at Castletown

While some of the landed gentry viewed life in the Irish countryside as a period of quiet boredom to be endured until their return to 'the town' for the Season, the Conollys always viewed time spent at Castletown as a welcome escape from the demands of urban social life. As Louisa stated in 1762: 'One is never so happy as when one is at home in the country'.[1] As the years progressed they increasingly opted to remain at home for as much of the Season as they could manage. This did not imply rural seclusion but rather that the socially mobile came to visit the Conollys at their grand spacious house in relative proximity to Dublin. With no children of their own to provide for, they indulged guests with fine wines, food and entertainments. Consequently, the majority of occasions for music and dancing at Castletown related to the entertainment of visitors. The house had been originally designed as a place of sociability with prominence being given to the main block of the house; utilitarian spaces like bedrooms, kitchens, and domestic offices were relegated to the wings. However, the enfilade of state apartments, located around the entrance hall and saloon, was more typical of the processional nature of early 18th-century formal sociability. By the latter half of the century, it was essential for guests to circulate, as in the assembly rooms, to partake in different activities occurring simultaneously in equally decorative rooms.[2]

The aim of the remodelling, refurbishment and redecoration works in the 1760s and 1770s was to take Castletown from a state of grand processional formality to a more informal circuit of comfortable and communal diversion. Louisa initially intended to tear down parts of the house but Emily's husband, then earl of Kildare, advised her that the project could proceed without doing so.[3] The state apartment, saloon and other formal reception rooms on the ground floor were reworked into a dining-room and decorated drawing-rooms. The double-height grand entrance hall area was enhanced with sumptuous stuccowork and by the addition of a magnificent cantilevered stone staircase. On the first floor, a long picture gallery was transformed into a lavishly decorated yet comfortable, informal and multifunctional space. There do not appear to have been designated rooms for music or dancing at Castletown. However, within the circuit of communal and diverting drawing-rooms, space could be requisitioned as necessary for the purposes of social dancing to music. This utilization of space provided optimal showcasing opportunities as the symbols of the wealth, position and pedigree of the family, including plate, portraits, artworks and furnishings, adorned these rooms. Louisa noticed the 'fine French glasses' and 'pretty French things' displayed at balls in the homes of her friends and it is clear that she followed suit at Castletown.[4] One of the rooms which might have been contemporaneously seen as a representative statement of the Conollys' lives and interests was the print room located on the ground floor, a former antechamber to the state bedroom that Louisa transformed by pasting on the walls an arrangement of printed engravings and etchings. Many of these were images of rural and hunting scenes, depictions of classical and religious subjects, and portraits of family members and influential figures known to the family. Theatre and literature were represented in some of the most prominent images with Louisa's favourite actor, Garrick, featuring in the centrepieces on the east and west walls. Music featured incidentally in a small number of images, probably chosen for their portrayal of domestic harmony, and in a series of ornamental trophies depicting musical instruments.[5]

The surviving household account books are replete with references to the items purchased to furnish the various rooms at Castletown, to the tradesmen and craftsmen charged with their decoration and to the numerous labourers engaged in remodelling works. These works curtailed the hosting of large assemblies, such as balls, particularly in the 1760s. Nevertheless, Louisa was still required to play her role as a hostess in the domiciliary sociability that was such a major part of Irish cultural life. Balls, for which invitations were issued, were usually organized in a country house when there was an important guest to be entertained or a significant family celebration such as a christening, a child's birthday, a coming-of-age or wedding. In the absence of such occasions, the Conollys entertained friends and relatives at their pleasure. Louisa's letters to Sarah reveal that, in the early 1760s, she was hosting large balls not at Castletown but in Dublin. It is not entirely clear where these balls occurred as the Conollys did not own a Dublin town house; they were renting a house on Merrion Street belonging to the 4th Earl Fitzwilliam by the 1770s. They also spent a lot of time at Kildare, later Leinster, House, the town house of the FitzGeralds, so it is possible that they hosted some events there. In any case, it was not unusual for them to host more than one ball in a week, as in April 1761, when Louisa remarked to Sarah: 'are we not mightily genteel to give two?'[6]

In spite of the ongoing refurbishment and remodelling works the Conollys were also entertaining company at Castletown itself as early as 1759. The FitzGeralds were invariable visitors and some of the children stayed for lengthy periods of time. Regular visitors included neighbouring landed gentry and clergymen, such as Revd Richard Marlay (1726–1802) of Celbridge Abbey, afterwards dean of Ferns and later bishop of Waterford.[7] In 1762, Louisa was able to boast to Sarah: 'we have had some very pleasant parties here'.[8] The basis of these house-parties, as observed by Mark Girouard, was that after breakfast guests were 'left to a considerable extent to do what they liked' until they convened for dinner.[9] This type of domiciliary sociability was particularly important for women of the nobility and gentry who did not have available to them the range of social outlets that men had. In Dublin or London, men had parliament as well as various clubs and public houses and in the country they had numerous outdoor pursuits. While women also took outdoor exercise such as walking and horse-riding, they were predominantly diverted indoors by reading, letter-writing, sketching, painting and needlework or 'working', as well as playing musical instruments and an 18th-century version of badminton known as 'battledore and shuttlecock'.[10] At Castletown, Louisa felt socially obligated to facilitate these activities, many of which occurred in the former picture gallery on the first floor. She told her sister Emily in October 1774 that she had, yet again, done 'the civil thing in having women here, which has been but tiresome but, however, is over'.[11]

Dining seems to have been the focus of much of the sociability at Castletown in the early years, even before the new dining-room was completed around 1767.[12] Dining was a domiciliary ritual that necessitated a designated room, formal dress, pre-dinner assembly and processional procedures. Music was sometimes provided during the meal and dancing may have occurred in an impromptu manner thereafter.[13] Dinner was not attended by visitors without invitation as this was considered familiar, forward and 'quite disgusting', as Louisa put it.[14] After dinner, the company usually retired upstairs to the long gallery which was lit by hundreds of candles reflecting repeatedly in the mirrors hanging on the walls. Louisa reported to Emily that it was 'the most comfortable room you ever saw, and quite warm; supper at one end, the company at the other, and I am writing in one of the piers at a distance from them all'.[15] This statement was not simply domestic pride on Louisa's part; the gallery was an exceptional room remarked upon by all visitors to Castletown.[16] Although very large, it was reportedly comfortable and organized in such a way that different types of activity could take place simultaneously in different areas of the room. Lady Caroline Dawson (1750–1813), afterwards the countess of Portarlington, wrote to her sister after a visit in 1778:

> But what struck me most was a gallery, I daresay 150 feet long, furnished in the most delightful manner with fine glasses, books, musical instruments, billiard table, in short, everything that you can think of is in that room, and though so large, is so well filled, that it is the warmest, most comfortable-looking place I ever saw; and they tell me they live in it quite in the winter, for the servants can bring in dinner or supper at one end, without anybody hearing it at the other.[17]

This type of description suggests that the room was extraordinary, not only for its beauty but, for its communal utility. While the arrangement of the furniture implied multiplicity of purpose, it also implied informality in the nature of the activities which occurred there. It was carefully furnished with placed chairs, sofas, bookshelves and mirrors as well as items conducive to relaxed diversion.

It was also favourable to the staging of amateur theatricals which were performed at Castletown by the Conollys and their friends as early as 1760.[18] Among the Castletown productions was a version of Shakespeare's *Henry IV, Part I* (1598) to which was added a prologue by the political and legal orator, Walter Hussey Burgh (1742–83).[19] Burgh and his wife were part of the Conollys' literary and theatrical circle that also included the FitzGerald family, neighbouring landlords such as Lord Russborough, clergymen such as Dean Marlay, members of the Gardiner, Macartney and Greville families and the Irish dramatist and poet Robert Jephson (1737–1803). Throughout the 1770s and 1780s Castletown hosted readings of various new literary works, some of which were dedicated to Louisa Conolly by friends and admirers. She also penned verses; her 'Inscription for the cottage at Castletown' featured in a miscellany of poems and songs published in London in 1799.[20]

The activities of the Conollys' literary circle also included singing and the playing of music. Louisa reported to her sisters in the 1770s that Mrs Elizabeth Gardiner (d. 1783) played the harpsichord and that Mr Fulke Greville (1717–1806) played the fiddle for the amusement of company at Castletown.[21] Given this company, it is likely that music and singing featured in the amateur theatrical productions put on there. Dancing may also have featured as it did in at least one production, in which the Conollys acted, at Carton in the 1760s. Among the Carton productions were versions of popular ballad-operas such as John Gay's *The beggar's opera* (1728) and *The devil to pay* (1732) by the Irish playwright Charles Coffey (*c.*1700–45). Although it is possible that the Carton versions were spoken-only adaptations, the choice of well-known musical pastiches of songs hints that at least some of the parts might have been sung.[22]

As works on the primary reception rooms at Castletown were progressing well in the late 1760s, Louisa found herself 'growing very lazy' and disliked going into Dublin, even when society demanded it.[23] In the summer of 1767 Thomas Conolly took, what his wife termed, 'a delightful frisk' of throwing balls for the FitzGerald children. This is the context within which the earliest reference to a ball at Castletown is found in Thomas's personal account book. The entry, for 28 July 1767, reads 'paid fiddlers for three different balls, £19 6s. 9d.'[24] The amount paid suggests that a number of fiddlers played at each ball. Louisa told her sister Sarah that she was 'monstrously obliged' to Thomas for employing them because she liked to make her nieces happy 'and a ball here does please them vastly because we have so good a room for dancing'.[25] It is not clear which room Louisa was referring to, but because a ball was always an opportunity for display, the largest and most impressive available room was the most likely space for dancing. Some of the adjoining rooms would have been suitably fitted up for card-playing, refreshments and smaller non-dancing groups of people.[26]

By the summer of 1772, Louisa was able to boast that she and Thomas had become 'the gayest of all people in this neighbourhood'.[27] Two balls were held at Castletown in the month of August, the 'musick' for which cost the Conollys £13 13s., an amount which suggests that a band of musicians played on each occasion. So large was the crowd that, at a cost of £6 16s. 6d., servants were borrowed from the duke of Leinster to wait on guests.[28] At least one of these balls was given for Lady Emily FitzGerald who told her aunt that 'she never enjoyed one more, nor ever had dancing enough before'. Louisa reported to Sarah that about 100 people attended, which was 'no crowd in this house', and that the dancing went on for almost four hours before supper and three hours thereafter. While the duchess of Leinster played cards with a group of older ladies, Louisa danced so much that she was 'quite jaded' the following day. Indeed, the purpose of the ball seems to have been to enable the FitzGerald girls to practice their dancing. Emily was reported to have 'much improved' as a result of the ball while her younger sister Lady Charlotte Fitzgerald (1758–1836) reportedly danced 'minuets and country dances vastly well'.[29]

Louisa, as evidenced by her letters to her sisters, was more discerning about dancing than she was about music or singing. Although she subscribed mostly to dramatic, poetic or literary works during her lifetime, she did make a subscription to a publication on dancing as early as the 1760s: *Critical observations on the art of dancing; to which is added a collection of cotillons or French dances*. Written by the Italian choreographer and impresario Giovanni Andrea Gallini (1728–1805) and published in London in 1766, this was essentially a history of the form and function of dancing in different parts of the world, to which was appended a collection of cotillons. A cotillon was a type of 'contredanse', or refined country-dance, which had travelled from France and gained huge popularity in England and Ireland by the late 18th century. It was usually danced in a square formation by four couples.[30] Gallini's publication detailed the various figures of each cotillon and included the music to which each cotillon was to be danced.

The ability to appreciate music that was not accompanied by dancing or singing caused Louisa some concern, particularly after she was treated to musical concerts at Goodwood in England during the 1770s. The duke of Richmond had seemingly acquired a 'passion for music' after his marriage in 1757, something which surprised Louisa for she 'never thought it possible that he could like a concert'.[31] Musing on the subject in a letter to Sarah she wrote:

I do divert myself with the idea of my brother being such a *connoisseur* in music. I think it is a lucky thing his having acquired this taste for it, for it is an additional amusement to himself, and then it must be so pleasant to the duchess as she is so fond of it. And the entertainments at Goodwood, in consequence of it, will please his country neighbours, which is always a desirable thing to do.[32]

As well as concerts, Louisa hoped that a ball would be thrown at Goodwood in the spring of 1772, not only to please her while she was visiting, but because 'it would please the Chichester people, and that is a right thing to do'.[33]

For Louisa, the derivation of personal amusement from domiciliary music and dancing was of secondary relevance to the maintenance of social relations in the neighbourhood. So from 1768, when Thomas was elected as the MP for the duke of Richmond's borough of Chichester, the Conollys regularly attended assemblies and balls there. It was, according to Louisa, necessary to 'go and do civil things by the Chichester folks'.[34] Nonetheless, she was clearly aware of a distinction between the types of music that she enjoyed at the assembly room or the playhouse and the concerts of 'Italian music' enjoyed by the duke of Richmond. The duke's enthusiasm for this type of music seems to have been shared by Thomas Conolly – as evidenced by Louisa's letter to him from Goodwood in April 1772:

> The Miss Warings are here, and two musical men, so that we have a good deal of music – which I believe in time I should grow to like better than I do now. They are all very obliging and let themselves down to songs not worthy of them to please my bad taste in music. I often wish that you were here. I think you, would be so much amused, who love music.[35]

While Louisa preferred singing to instrumental music, she clearly preferred popular theatre songs to the more complex songs from operas, known as arias. This calls into question a subscription which she made in the later 1770s to a three-volume collection of songs arranged by Domenico Corri (1746–1825). Corri was a singing-master, composer and manager of the Theatre Royal in Edinburgh. His collection included 'the most admired' songs from 'operas in the highest esteem' to which were added simple bass accompaniments, written out in such a way as 'to enable any harpsichord player to accompany himself with ease'.[36] There is no evidence to suggest that Louisa could actually play the harpsichord; she opted to learn to play the English guitar, an easier instrument, at Blackrock in 1768. Her subscription to Corri's collection would appear, then, to have been a social duty, shared by the other society ladies whose names appeared in the subscription list. Interestingly, Louisa attributed her inclination towards popular songs to a natural impediment, rather than a disinclination towards, what she perceived as, the musical respectability espoused by the duke and duchess of Richmond. She wrote to Sarah:

> I wonder if it is possible for me <u>ever</u> to acquire such a taste. My brother having done it makes me think that perhaps I might. Though I have often tried, I never found that I could like Italian music. I have a notion that it is owing to some fault in the formation of my ear that sounds strike me differently from what they do other people, and, if so, I can never grow to like it.[37]

Regardless of her musical preferences or abilities, aiming to please others was evidently Louisa's comprehension of the purpose of music and dancing as domiciliary entertainments.

Aiming to please would be the object of the entertainments hosted at Castletown; not only for the maintenance of good relations with neighbours, friends and relatives but also with servants and tenants. Music and dancing were not the preserve of the upper classes as the agriculturalist Arthur Young noted in the 1770s. 'The poor people, both men and women, learn to dance and are exceedingly fond of amusement', he wrote, 'the love of dancing and musick are almost universal amongst them'.[38] While staying at Blackrock, Louisa herself witnessed 'the country people dance minuets and jigs, and surprisingly well' at a servants' wedding.[39] The first rare reference to a 'servants ball' in the Castletown accounts relates to October 1772, when a fiddler named Meehan was paid 11s. 4½d. for his services.[40]

Servants in the Irish country house were usually given a dinner and a ball at Christmas time and at significant family celebrations. Among the tenantry on the estate, weddings and comings-of-age were also usually celebrated but, in the absence of such occasions at Castletown, traditional festivities, such as the saving of the harvest, were marked instead.[41] This is not immediately evident from the household accounts which, although meticulously written up by Louisa herself, often reflected amalgamated payments on a quarter-year basis. It is not until September 1800, when a fiddler named Crawley was paid 5s. 5d. 'for playing at the harvest dance', that a further specific reference to such an entertainment is found.[42] Those attending a harvest dance at Castletown would have been entertained, based on their social status, somewhere between the house and tents pitched for the occasion on the demesne. The entertaining of the lower orders was typical of some contemporary English country houses where the landed gentry were becoming increasingly occupied with life in the country.[43]

The engagement of the Irish landowning gentry with country life was reflected in the growing popularity of outdoor diversions. Fox-hunting was particularly popular during the season, from November until April. Hunts were usually hosted in rotation among landowners in a particular area and the attendant entertainments of music, dancing and dining could last for up to a week. Thomas Conolly had a well-established pack of fox-hounds and hosted many hunts on the Castletown estate.[44] Musical entertainment was provided for the hunt not only in the grand mansion but also at other venues on the estate. In 1781, for instance, an anonymous piper was paid 11s. 4½d. for playing at Leinster Lodge, the Conollys' hunting lodge.[45] Among the guests who enjoyed the fox-hunting at Castletown in the 1760s and 1770s were successive lords lieutenant, each of whom brought an entourage, including at least two aides-de-camp. Aides-de-camp were usually considered to be good dancers and were very much in demand as dancing partners at all types of events.[46] They were among the guests who stayed at Castletown for three weeks between Christmas 1775 and January 1776, when the guest of honour was the outgoing lord lieutenant Simon Harcourt (1714–77), 1st Earl Harcourt. Louisa wrote to Emily, now the dowager duchess of Leinster:

> Our gallery was in great vogue, and really is a charming room, for there are such variety of occupations in it that people cannot be formal in it. Lord Harcourt was writing, some of us played at whist, others at billiards, Mrs Gardiner at the harpsichord, others at work, others at chess, others reading, and supper at one end; all this without interruption to the different occupations. I have seldom seen twenty people in a room so easily disposed of.[47]

In the middle of 1776, the Conollys were beginning to feel the physical toll of this sociability. Louisa told Emily: 'Mr Conolly and I begin to feel that we are not quite as young as we were, and don't like so much company as we are obliged to see here.'[48]

By 1777, however, they would be elevated to a position of social prominence in Ireland greater than ever before: Thomas's brother-in-law, John Hobart (1723–93), the 2nd earl of Buckinghamshire, was appointed as the new lord lieutenant. Being thus related (and because the Buckinghamshires did 'not know a soul') the Conollys were obliged to guide the lord lieutenant and his wife in their animation and arbitration of fashionable Dublin society.[49] For the first time in many years Thomas and Louisa did not make their annual trip to London for the Season. Instead they went to Dublin to make preparations for the arrival of the lord lieutenant, his wife and daughter. They were evidently concerned with making a good impression at the multitude of social events that they would be expected to attend over the coming years. Thomas's personal account book shows that in June 1777, the considerable sum of £29 11s. 6d. was paid for six months of dancing lessons from a Mr Williams.[50] At Castletown, they were bombarded with all sorts of requests for recommendations for offices of one kind or another. Louisa spent hours in the long gallery responding to 'the millions of applications' made to her by tradesmen and friends alike, none of which she could oblige.[51]

Despite the intensification of social obligation, Louisa was enthused about the possibility of 'leading so much a pleasanter a life' at Castletown in 1777. The lord lieutenant himself was a regular visitor particularly when he needed 'to rest from his fatigues'.[52] Indeed, as a result of the Conollys' relationship with Buckinghamshire, and having a well-established tradition of entertaining lords lieutenant, Castletown now became *the* centre of domiciliary hospitality and sociability in Ireland. A number of entertainments were held there in the summer of 1777, the 'musick' for which cost the Conollys £21 15s.[53] Among these was 'a very pretty illumination' held in the woods behind the house which was accompanied by a masquerade ball.[54] Usually associated with royal spectacles and city life, an outdoor illumination using oil-lamps and, perhaps, transparencies with colours and shapes thereon, would have been quite an extraordinary undertaking.

By 1780, the Conollys were fully committed to life in Ireland as Thomas ceased to represent Chichester in the English house of commons. Winter continued to be the most socially demanding part of the year at Castletown particularly in the period between Christmas and New Year's Day. The household account books show that all sorts of goods, foodstuffs and alcohol were delivered to the house for the festivities and that musicians were always employed. Lack of consistency or detail in the account book entries, however, makes it difficult to determine the number of events at which musicians were employed and the number of musicians employed for any specific event. However, fiddlers and pipers did usually feature and the music provided by them was usually for the purpose of social dancing.

While their time at Castletown centred on improving and charitable activities, estate management and hospitality, the Conollys were still expected to participate in the hectic round of entertainments that accompanied the Dublin Season. Louisa attended many of these in her capacity as chaperone to a number of young society ladies including the lord lieutenant's 15-year-old daughter Harriet Hobart (1762–1805). The Conollys were now prominent theatre patrons and Harriet was taken to see numerous actors including the celebrated Richard Brinsley Sheridan (1751–1816) who performed to 'a very full house' at Crow Street. Theatre in Dublin appears to have been particularly noteworthy at this time with Thursday becoming 'the fashionable night for going to the play'. That music continued to feature in plays seen by Louisa is evidenced by her report to Emily that for 'the singing, Mr Webster, Miss Potter, and Miss Barsanti are (I am told) excellent; so that we are well off … it's a pretty diversion'.[55] Diversion as opposed to edification was, for Louisa, the merit of many these plays.

The operas being produced in Dublin theatres in 1777 were also considered 'charming' and 'better than any they have had in London for some years past'.[56] It was around this time that Thomas Conolly played a role in kick-starting the career of the singer, actor, composer and theatrical manager, Michael Kelly (1762–1826). From a young age Kelly received piano lessons from a number of teachers, including Philip Cogan (c.1748–1833), who was also employed by the Conollys to teach their niece Louisa Staples. He also received singing lessons from the numerous Italian singers employed in Dublin's entertainment venues. Kelly unexpectedly made his stage-debut at the Smock Alley theatre in Dublin when the Italian castrato, Gaspero Savoi (d. 1792), engaged there took ill. There was no male soprano substitute to sing in the opera 'La buona figliuola' ['The good girl'] but the attention of the opera company was directed to 15-year-old Kelly. Although his father initially refused to permit him to perform, the company manger prevailed upon Thomas Conolly, who was in the audience with the 2nd duke of Leinster, to persuade him otherwise. Kelly proved a great success and he went on to have a remarkable international career as a tenor. He became a friend of Wolfgang Amadeus Mozart (1756–91) and was one of the leading figures in British theatre around the turn of the 19th century.[57]

While the theatres seem to have led the way in terms of new music, Dublin Castle, being 'now quite the fashionable place', led when it came to dancing. In November 1777, for instance, Louisa reported to the dowager duchess of Leinster that 'a new kind of minuet' had recently been introduced there. Although she thought that this '*minuet de la cour*', demonstrated by Mr Corbet, an aide-de-camp, was 'vastly pretty' she was not convinced about the content: 'I don't think it a minuet neither, for there are *entre chats* in it.'[58] (An *entre chat* was a step during which the dancer crossed the legs a number of times, alternately back and forth.) This further highlights Louisa's confidence in making judgments on dancing; her statements on music were always qualified by the words: 'I am told'.

Louisa was certainly confident in her own abilities as a hostess at Castletown by 1778, telling Sarah that all her 'little amusements' were 'so flourishing' that she did not leave home 'without some good reason'.[59] One of the intended amusements in July 1778 was another illumination that fell victim to the weather, as Louisa reported to Emily: 'it turned out (as it generally does) a rainy evening, so that it ended in a ball in the house, which I thought very hot and disagreeable, but the company seemed to enjoy themselves.'[60] The illumination seems to have gone ahead later in the year, the entertainments for which included music by a fiddler named Higgins and two large barrels of ale at a cost of £2 18s.[61] Among the guests at these entertainments were some of the most celebrated professional actors of the day.

The appearance of John Henderson (1745–85) and Frances Abington (1737–1815) at a dinner and ball at Castletown in 1778 drew criticism from some quarters, as Louisa incredulously told her sister Emily: 'I have been abused in the newspapers for having them, which is too ridiculous.' The dowager duchess of Leinster responded by scolding Louisa for allowing her daughter Charlotte, then in the Conollys' care, to be seen keeping the company of a paid actress in particular. Louisa defended her decision to invite the actors to Castletown, having found them 'both vastly well-behaved and agreeable'. However, while she insisted that 'it was quite genteel to invite Mrs Abington', she promised Emily that she would not let Charlotte be seen in her company again.[62]

The Buckinghamshire viceroyalty ended in 1780 and Louisa told Sarah that she was 'very glad that our reign is over'.[63] The Conollys had acquired more acquaintances than they could visit with pleasure and continued to encourage people to visit them. In fact, they now had 'a sort of public day on Sunday' when people were received.[64] This 'public' aspect of life at Castletown is further evidenced by the presence there of what Louisa called 'a coffee-room'.[65] While the keeping of such a room at Castletown was considered 'a wicked thing' by Lady Powerscourt in 1762, it was now considered to be 'in the most modern elegant taste', and the Conollys' mode of living 'in the highest style of hospitality'. It was described by a visitor in 1778 as 'a public news or coffee-room, for the common resort of his guests in boots, where he who goes away early may breakfast, or he who comes in late may dine, or he who would choose to go to bed, may sup before the rest of the family. This is, almost, princely'.[66]

Throughout the 1780s, 'princely' Castletown played a central role in domiciliary sociability in Ireland. While music and dancing continued to feature in the entertainment of guests, there was also a more informal aspect to these activities, as Thomas wrote to his brother-in-law: 'our gallery is full, some singing, some playing at chess, others at cards, in short making so much noise that I must conclude this'.[67] Louisa entertained, what she considered, 'very agreeable' company at Castletown during these years. There were regular visitors, like the Jephsons, Grevilles, Marlays and FitzGeralds, and others like the prominent army officer General John Burgoyne (1722–92). Burgoyne was also an accomplished playwright and, in many ways, embodied the two types of male visitors to Castletown during the 1780s and 1790s: literary men and military men. While the literary presence had been there from the outset the military presence reflected more recent developments.[68]

The outbreak of war between Britain and the colonies in North America had necessitated a withdrawal of regular government troops from Ireland after 1775. A threat of foreign invasion was sparked in 1778 with the open declaration of war on Britain by France in alliance with the colonies. This brought into being in Ireland an armed civilian force, organized into small corps, raised by local initiative, commanded and paid for by prominent members of the landed gentry. The duke of Leinster was the first commander-in-chief of these volunteers.[69] For his part, Thomas Conolly was responsible for the Castletown Union Volunteers; dinners held for this unit ranged in cost from £9 8s. 8½d. in April 1780 to £21 8s. 2d. in June 1781.[70] The general intensification of military activity, both at home and abroad, was felt at Castletown. As well as being involved with the volunteers, many friends and relatives of the Conollys served in the British army and navy in America. Uniformed officers and military aides-de-camp regularly attended as guests at social gatherings at Castletown. Military men were sometimes involved in providing the music. For an event at Castletown in August 1780, for instance, the Conollys paid a sum of £9 2s. for a combination of musicians including an 'artillery band', two fiddlers and a number of pipers.[71] Although raised to assist in the defence of the country, the foreign threat was not realized and the volunteers became a political movement declaring for various economic and political liberties. They grew increasingly militant and, aligned with the campaign led by Henry Grattan (1746–1820), brought such extra-parliamentary pressure to bear that a measure of Irish legislative independence was achieved in 1782.

While the volunteers became less influential after the end of the war in America in 1783, their presence was still felt in Irish social life. Colourful parades of uniformed men, choreographed military reviews and other ceremonial spectacles became part of the cultural milieu in the latter part of the 18th century.[72] Some volunteer units had substantial bands comprising players of woodwind, brass and percussion instruments who provided music for marching and ceremonial purposes. By the 1790s, military bands had grown in such popularity that they began to be utilized in a variety of social contexts. As well as marching music the repertory tended to include arrangements of the popular concert, operatic and other theatre music of the day. It is not known if the Castletown Union Volunteers had a band as such but Thomas Conolly's personal and household account books show that there was a fifer and a drummer in his pay from about 1780. It was typical for an infantry corps to be accompanied by young non-combatant fifers and drummers. The role of the drummer was to assist in maintaining formation and rhythm while marching. The fifer, playing a small but high-pitched flute, was particularly useful in providing military signals and could also play tunes to entertain the men. As well providing uniforms for these boys, Thomas paid a local family by the name of Stuart for their 'lodging and dieting'. Evidently concerned with their general education, he also paid for them to be taught to read and write by the local school schoolmaster John Walsh.[73] Information about their musical instruction, if they received any, is not known. The drummer was in Thomas's employ until January 1787, while the fifer remained until, at least, 1796.[74]

Sociability at Castletown was not curbed by the militarization of social and cultural life in the 1780s; in fact, it seems to have been invigorated. Successive lords lieutenant were still happy to entertain and be entertained at Castletown as the house was now generally considered as 'the finest in the kingdom'.[75] The viceroyalty of Charles Manners (1754–87), the 4th duke of Rutland, marked a particularly sociable period in Dublin and at Castletown. According to Louisa 'nothing ever was so gay as the neighbourhood' in those years. Members of the Clements family were particular friends of the Conollys and their house at Killadoon, near Celbridge, was occasionally used to accommodate guests attending entertainments at Castletown.[76] The Clements family also accommodated the vice-regal administration in their quest for a suitable residence by selling to them their Ranger's Lodge in the Phoenix Park in the early 1780s. Although remodelling and redecoration would curtail sociability there for some years, the duchess of Rutland, being keen to establish herself in Ireland as a social hostess, threw a large ball there in December 1786. Controversially, Louisa only received a last-minute invitation after the duchess had been prompted to invite her but she attended, nonetheless, as chaperone to her niece Harriette Staples. Louisa's letters reveal that she did not hold the young duchess in any esteem.[77] She complained to her sister Emily that she would now be 'obliged to ask her to some of our little dances'.[78] Many of these dances were held during the hunting season which continued to be, as Louisa put it to Sarah, 'the season when the house is full of company'.[79]

The winter of 1786 seems to have been particularly busy at Castletown 'in consequence of some very good hunting'. In December, Louisa reported 'a houseful of fox-hunters' and some French gentlemen that the Conollys had met at Carton. The Jephsons read a new play shortly to be produced in London. By Christmas-time, the house was so crowded with guests that Louisa, who desired to invite some of her closest friends to a ball, could 'not offer them beds'.[80] Louisa's sister Sarah, who was also visiting, reported:

> Castletown goes on as usual, always the receptacle for society, comfort, and friendship, and very often for innumerable personages – some old, some young, some agreeable, and some very intolerable. The Christmas is the general rendezvous of the nobility, gentry, and mobility here. It was very full and very sociable, which is uncommon in a large company, but the Long Gallery divides the party so much one is capable of being very quiet at one end, though there is dancing at the other.[81]

Although it may have been spurred on by competition from the Rutlands at the new vice-regal lodge, Christmas 1786 marked the zenith of sociability at Castletown, particularly in terms of the scale and lavishness of entertainments on offer.

The household account books attest to the remarkable seasonal revelries which, of course, included music and dancing. 24 pounds of chocolate were imported from 'Mr Twining in London' at a cost £6 0s. 4d. while £7 6s. 3d. was paid 'at the time of the ball' for the services of a French cook, Mr Castro, and his apprentice. A sum of £5 13s. 9d. was paid to an unnamed piper for playing at 'the X'mas party', £9 2s. was paid to a 'band of musicians for ditto' and £3 8s. 3d. 'to the musicians at the ball'. There was clearly a distinction here between 'the X'mas party' and 'the ball'.[82] The ball was evidently a more formal event to which invitations were issued, while the party would have been a more informal occasion for music and dancing in the long gallery. The arrangement of furniture in the gallery would not have been favourable to dancing on any grand scale but there was probably space for small country-dance formations.

These Christmas festivities were replicated at Castletown the following year. In January 1788 Louisa told her sister Emily: 'I was obliged to write cards of invitation to a very little ball that we had here on Wednesday, and to take some trouble about the dinner and supper of that day.'[83] The music for the ball cost £5 13s. 9d., which included the travel expenses of musicians from Dublin.[84] The guests were as numerous as ever and included members of the household of the new lord lieutenant, George Nugent-Temple-Grenville (1753–1813), the 1st marquis of Buckingham. Things were very different by 1789, however, as the politics of Thomas Conolly clashed with those of Buckingham's administration. During the Regency crisis of 1788–9, when George III was incapacitated by one of the temporary bouts of insanity to which he was prone, the Irish parliament voted to offer the regency of Ireland to the Prince of Wales as advocated by the reforming Whigs at Westminster. However, Buckingham refused to make the recommendation and Conolly, as one of the chief Irish advocates, was removed from an office that he held on the Board of Trade.[85] Consequently, the Conollys withdrew from attending social events at the vice-regal court and successive lords lieutenant avoided visiting Castletown during the 1790s.

While Castletown remained one of the most prominent venues for domiciliary hospitality outside of the new vice-regal lodge, there was a perceptible shift in the nature of sociability there. This reflected a number of developments in the lives of the Conollys including a shift in the nature of Thomas Conolly's company, for although he had fallen out of favour with the government in Ireland his political influence had grown in other respects. In 1790, he was a founder-member of the Whig Club, to promote administrative and economic reforms. He was an active member hosting dinners and making speeches which were widely reported in patriot newspapers. Occasions for music and dancing continued to be provided for guests at Castletown: at Christmas 1790, for instance, the Conollys hired 'a band of music' at a price of £5 13s. 9d. and a fiddler named Crawley for 11s. 4½d.[86] However, Thomas was inconsistent in his political views and inextricably linked with prominent

Tory politicians and government supporters including the duke of Richmond. Following the outbreak of war between Britain and revolutionary France in 1793, Thomas voted with the government on the formation of a new defence militia, led by the landed gentry, and was rewarded with the colonelcy of the Londonderry regiment.[87] This militia regiment was often entertained at the home of its commander which was now well-established as 'the residence of true Irish hospitality'.[88]

Moves to renew social relations between Castletown and Dublin Castle were made in the summer of 1795. Louisa wrote to the wife of the new lord lieutenant, John Jeffreys Pratt (1759–1840), the 2nd earl Camden, to explain that 'the unfortunate state of politics precludes me from the honour of waiting upon your ladyship as our vice-queen'.[89] Lady Camden responded by expressing the hope that political differences would not prevent them from meeting. Louisa replied that she looked forward to this, not at Castletown but, 'at some of our friends' houses'.[90] By this time, Ireland was in a state of serious civil unrest and Castletown did not go unaffected. In July 1795, Louisa had 'got all the arms ready and loaded' and put the house 'into a state of defence' owing to agitation by a group of 'Defenders' around Celbridge.[91] The outbreak of rebellion in 1798 was difficult for the Conollys as they had relatives on both the government and the rebel sides. 'We are plunged into a most dreadful civil war', wrote Louisa to the duke of Richmond, in June 1798. 'Wexford is the worst, the county of Kildare next, in which we live, and we are surrounded by different posts of the insurgents.' As much as Louisa tried to maintain a sense of normality, the house was no longer conducive to sociability: 'we have 18 soldiers sleeping in our drawing-rooms ... and a sentinel constantly on the roof of the house'.[92] Castletown was now a garrison.

By the late 1790s, there were fewer occasions for music and dancing at Castletown than previously. There were none of the grand formal balls, with bands of musicians and luxury foods, witnessed in the 1780s. In fact, after 1798, Castletown declined as a centre of hospitality, entertainment and sociability. As agents in the entertainment of important social, political and military figures, music and dancing also suffered a decline. This is not to say, however, that music or dancing ceased to function in the lives of the Conollys. Over the years, they were entrusted with the care and education of numerous young relatives, some of whom became long-term residents at Castletown. Music and dancing continued to function there in terms of domestic music-making by these young people and in terms of their social edification.

3. Masters, musicians and music tradesmen

Two of the Conollys' relatives who become long-term residents at Castletown were the Staples sisters: Louisa Anne (*c*.1767–1833) and Henrietta (Harriette) Margaret (1770–1847). Nieces of Thomas Conolly, the girls were sent from Lissan, Co. Tyrone, to be reared at Castletown after their mother died in 1771. Louisa Conolly's stated mission for the girls, from their very arrival, was to begin with their education. She was frightened by this, having no children of her own, but was confident that she would do a much better job than any member of the Staples family, whom she considered 'vulgar'.[1] Louisa felt that the 'great point' of education was 'to find out the real character' of a child and 'then to assist it'.[2] This meant socializing a child, making her comfortable and confident around other children, teaching her how to behave appropriately in various situations and correcting her 'disagreeable ways'.[3] She took the Staples girls to the theatres in Dublin from a very young age and encouraged them to perform their own plays. She ensured that they were taught basic reading, writing and arithmetic by governesses at Castletown. After some years, specialist 'masters' were employed to instruct them in various subjects such as drawing, geography, the French and Italian languages as well as music and dancing. Louisa was firmly of the opinion that all of these things were 'well worth acquiring' as part of a good education.[4]

At the same time, the Conollys were also acting *in loco parentis* for some of the FitzGerald children. The 1st duke of Leinster had died in November 1773 and his widow Emily had eloped to France with her sons' tutor William Ogilvie (1740–1832). Some of the younger children stayed at Castletown for months on end while Louisa prepared the older ones for their debuts in society. She took pride in ensuring that her charges performed well and were admired in all social situations. Naturally, then, it was to the Conollys at Castletown that William, the 2nd duke of Leinster, presented his new wife, Emilia St George (*c*.1753–1798) in 1775. Having prepared the new duchess of Leinster for a ball at Dublin Castle, Louisa was pleased to report, to the dowager duchess, that her dancing was 'really the finest thing I ever saw; 'tis the most perfect, graceful minuet that a woman of fashion can dance … She does seem to have all the *sang froid* about it that I used to have at twelve years old, vastly taken up with the thoughts of performing well, but no shame'.[5]

Dancing was a particularly significant accomplishment for a woman as it indicated an investment in her social refinement and, thereby, pointed to her background. In order to participate fully in society events, and be admired for that participation, one was expected to be able to dance. Instruction often began as early as seven years of age and continued, at least, until marriage. There was often an intensification of instruction prior to the debut or formal presentation at court. Dancing at the debutante ball was the culmination of years of preparatory lessons not only in dance steps but also in grace, courtesy and deportment. It was, in many respects, a statement of merit as a marriage partner. While a woman did not necessarily require a dancing-master after marriage, some women continued to take lessons in order to maintain their acquired standard and to learn new dances. It is not entirely clear if the dancing-masters employed by the Conollys to instruct the Staples girls gave their lessons at Castletown or if the girls travelled to Dublin. It may have been a combination of both as the household account and receipt books show that payments were made to dancing-masters in both places. There are some references in Louisa's correspondence to the girls having gone 'to town to their masters' but the specialty is not stated.[6] Nonetheless, it can be said that, from the 1780s, the Conollys of Castletown were employers of the following dancing-masters: Mr J. Fontaine (1780–3), Mr J.B. Aubry (1783–8), Mr Wilson (1792) and Mr Grecco (1799–1800). It is difficult to locate biographical detail on these men but some interesting relevancies do emerge from the available sources.

Dancing-masters were usually literate men. Fontaine and Aubry signed for payments they received in French, indicating that they probably were of that nationality. Whether or not they taught in the house at Castletown or at a venue in Dublin, they probably played their own music on a 'kit' or pocket-violin as they taught the steps. All new pupils were charged an enrolment fee or 'entrance-money' by their dancing-master when they first began lessons with them. This usually cost £2 5s. 6d. and was applied by all of the masters associated with Castletown. Each time that a pupil changed to a new master, another enrolment fee had to be paid. While the standard price of a single dancing lesson was around 3s. 9½d., lessons were usually taught in blocks of 8 at a time.[7] Fontaine is the first of the Conollys' dancing-masters about whom we have any knowledge. Louisa Staples was taking regular sets of lessons with him for a number of months each year between 1780 and 1783. Louisa Conolly believed that for any young girl, 'two months learning each year would surely be sufficient to make her dance as much as is necessary and would be quite sufficient also for diversions'.[8] Like many professionals associated with music and dancing at the time, dancing-masters were not solely reliant on their income from dancing lessons. Fontaine was involved with producing and staging entertainments at theatres and assembly rooms in Dublin. In May 1789, for example, 'a grand concert of vocal and instrumental music' put on at the Exhibition Rooms on William Street by prominent musicians and singers, concluded with a ball 'conducted by Mr Fontaine'.[9]

Enterprising dancing-masters also found ways to capitalize on their association with the nobility and landed gentry. Advertisements for subscription balls conducted on Fontaine's own initiative which began 'Mr Fontaine begs leave to inform the nobility and gentry that …' were placed on the front pages of newspapers like the *Freeman's Journal*. Dancing lessons were used as opportunities to sell tickets to these balls and the revenue potential was maximized by selling single-admission tickets at a higher price. It was also relatively lucrative for the likes of Fontaine to promote his subscription balls as opportunities for young girls to exhibit their dancing, particularly in advance of debut presentations. Although girls who had not yet made their debut were precluded from attending formal non-domiciliary assemblies, they were permitted to attend certain preparatory events, particularly those organized by a dancing-master. Thus, Fontaine targeted his pupils and their guardians, highlighting that his balls were 'conducted in the genteelest manner'.[10] Children and unmarried women could not attend by themselves and, so, additional tickets were purchased for chaperones and family members. The Castletown account books show that the Conollys attended a number of balls given by Fontaine when Louisa Staples was his pupil in the early 1780s. She was making preparations for her presentation at Dublin Castle in November 1783.

As well as attending Fontaine's balls, Louisa also attended a number of domiciliary balls along with her companion Sophia FitzGerald (1762–1845). In the early 1780s Sophia and some of her siblings continued to live at Castletown, in the care of the Conollys, even though their mother, the dowager duchess of Leinster, had returned from France to live between Dublin and London. As noted, some of the balls held at Castletown in the 1770s were for the entertainment of these children but they also presented opportunities for budding debutantes to practice their dancing. This continued into the 1780s to encourage the socialization of the Staples girls. On any given evening at Castletown there was 'a tidy family party of twenty people' assembled for dinner and 'a little dance afterwards for the young folks'.[11] Musicians were engaged by the Conollys for these little dances; in September 1782, for example, they hired fiddlers at a cost of £2 16s. 9½d.[12] Hence, Sophia FitzGerald and Louisa Staples grew close and attended a variety of entertainments together including Lady Earlsfort's ball on Monday, 28 February 1783. Sophia noted in her journal that there was 'a great crowd, very disagreeable, the house beautiful. Stayed till near five o'clock … Only danced one dance after supper. Louisa did not seem to enjoy it'.[13] This was followed by the FitzGibbons' ball on Thursday, 10 March 1783, which the both girls found 'much pleasanter than Lady Earlsfort's. Stayed till past five o'clock in the morning'.[14] Later in that year, both girls attended the regular Maynooth ball, patronized by Sophia's brother, the duke of Leinster. It was not held in a domestic venue but at an inn in Maynooth, which 'was not very full for the inn-keeper, but enough so for the dancers, who seemed to enjoy it prodigiously'.[15]

Attending a ball anywhere required a lot of preparation, not only in terms of performance and behaviour but also with regard to dressing the hair and body. However, attending an event at the vice-regal court was bound by even more exacting etiquette and required appropriate court attire. Louisa Staples' presentation at Dublin Castle was postponed until January 1784 because her aunt did not think her 'prepared with clothes as yet'. In the meantime, she was required to continue with her preparations and was powdered for the first time to attend an evening party hosted by Mrs Pery. Louisa Conolly told her sister Emily she did not like 'a moment's idleness' for her niece and had her recommence lessons with all of her masters.[16]

Fontaine, however, had gone to Paris for the winter and, although he was only temporarily absent, a new dancing-master, Aubry, was acquired for Louisa Staples. The usual entrance-money was paid to him in November 1783. Louisa was joined in her dancing lessons by Harriette Staples who was thoroughly caught up in the excitement of preparations for her sister's debut at the Castle. These preparations were evidently a success as Louisa attracted the attention of a young naval officer, Thomas Pakenham (1757–1836), from Co. Westmeath. The Conollys no longer paid for her dancing lessons after her marriage to Pakenham in June 1785. This is not to say, however, that she did not have further lessons in order to maintain her acquired standard and to learn new dances. In 1802, she was persuaded by her aunt to dance at a ball at Castletown 'which she did merrily when once she began but was at first ashamed because of her ten children'.[17]

Harriette Staples continued until the late 1780s in her lessons with Aubry, who was also employed by the FitzGeralds at Carton.[18] Like Fontaine, he was involved in activities other than teaching. He held subscription balls at venues around Dublin that functioned in a similar way and for similar ends as those of Fontaine. The advertisements for these balls contained the usual deferential address to the nobility and gentry and highlighted 'the patronage of many ladies of distinction' as well as novelty performances by his pupils of 'fancy dances and new quadrilles'. Some advertisements emphasized Aubry's musical capabilities: 'N.B. The music and figure of the quadrilles are of Mr Aubry's composition; they will be played with wind instruments.'[19] Again, the Conollys patronized some of these events. The household accounts show that on 25 May 1787, for instance, Louisa paid Aubry £2 4s. 5d. for 'two gentlemen's tickets and four ladies tickets' to one of his balls, the gentlemen's tickets being the more expensive.[20]

Like her sister, Harriette Staples put her lessons to use from an early age. As well as attending entertainments conducted by her dancing-master she also attended an array of domiciliary entertainments. In December 1786, for example, she attended five different balls in the vicinity of Castletown. One of these was at the Clements' of Killadoon from which she and her aunt 'got away in very reasonable time, and were home by half an hour after three o'clock. The dancing lagged a little as there were rather too few dancers'.[21] Harriette was also at the duchess of Rutland's Christmas ball in the newly-acquired vice-regal lodge in the Phoenix Park. It was well-attended but 'not crowded' and she 'got partners for every dance'.[22] There is little evidence in the Castletown accounts of Harriette's dancing lessons after 1788 but this is not to say that, perhaps, her own father did not pay for her to continue with them. We find that she was dancing at a ball at Almack's in London, in March 1792, her admission fee of £1 1s. paid by the Conollys.[23] By 1796 Harriette Staples was married to the diplomat Richard Le Poer Trench (1767–1837), afterwards the 2nd earl of Clancarty; the Conollys, however, were definitely paying for her instruction in music up until her marriage.

Both of the Staples girls had been instructed in music while living at Castletown, where the following music-masters were employed: Dr Philip Cogan (1780), Mrs Jane Coffy (1781–5), Mr James Duncan (1785–7), Mr John Day (1789–96). As with the dancing-masters, it is difficult to locate biographical detail on some of these people but some general observations can be made. Music-masters were usually literate and signed for the payments that they received in English. Some, like Jane Coffy, were female. Whether or not they taught in the house at Castletown is not apparent but, like the dancing-masters, they charged all new pupils entrance-money of £2 5s. 6d. As with dancing, the standard price of a lesson in music was about 3s. 9½d. but lessons were always taught in blocks. Music-masters also supplied materials such as music sheets or 'music', music books, including 'sets of lessons', and 'ruled' music copy-books.[24]

Louisa Staples' first music-master, Philip Cogan, was particularly noteworthy. He was a highly regarded keyboard musician who lived in Dublin from 1772. He directed a number of theatre orchestras and regularly played as an organist or pianist at instrumental concerts. He was, for instance, one of the solo instrumentalists who performed as part of the concert which preceded Mr Fontaine's ball in May 1789 at the Exhibition Rooms. Like many musicians, Cogan supplemented his income through teaching; his pupils included the aforementioned tenor Michael Kelly and the poet Thomas Moore (1779–1852). In 1780, Louisa Staples received 24 lessons from him on the harpsichord at a cost of £4 11s.[25] Cogan also worked as a composer of stage works, songs, piano concertos and keyboard sonatas, some with violin accompaniments. Some of these were dedicated to a number of ladies of the nobility and gentry, including the duchess of Leinster. Apart from their general affection for the theatre and extensive patronage of concerts, this dedication suggests that Cogan might also have been teaching music to the FitzGeralds at Carton. However, he seems to have stopped teaching Louisa Staples around 1780, the year that he was appointed as the organist at St Patrick's Cathedral in Dublin.

Between 1781 and 1785, Louisa was instructed by Mrs Jane Coffy, who also taught her sister Harriette. Before her marriage to Thomas Pakenham in June 1785, however, Louisa had a new music-master in James Duncan. Duncan also became Harriette's music-master in 1787 but there seems to have been a hiatus in her lessons until 1789 when she was enrolled with John Day. Like many music-masters, Duncan and Day were probably theatre musicians who supplemented their income by teaching the children of the nobility and landed gentry. Duncan may have, in fact, been the featured pianist in an early 19th century orchestra led by Philip Cogan at the Rotunda.[26] In any case, it would appear that all of the music-masters employed by the Conollys gave instruction on keyboard instruments. Some of the entries in the Castletown account and tradesmen's receipts books specify harpsichord lessons in the 1780s but most entries simply state 'music'. It can be taken that some lessons would have been dedicated to the rudiments of reading music notation and others to its practical application. The purpose of such instruction is less apparent than that of instruction in dancing which was absolutely necessary for participation in society.

While it was acceptable for men of the nobility and landed gentry to practice in a non-domiciliary capacity as amateur musicians, for charitable or entertaining purposes, it was not usually so for women. Even in a domiciliary capacity, the women staying in a house like Castletown did not supply the music to accompany dancing at a ball. This was done by professional musicians and, although many of these remain anonymous, the household accounts allow some general conclusions to be drawn. It appears that small groups of fiddlers were the most common form of paid musical entertainment at Castletown in the late 18th century, presumably because they played the most suitable music for dancing. Fiddlers were sometimes accompanied by players of other instruments, such as the dulcimer, a stringed-instrument played by striking with small hammers. This particular combination was hired at Castletown for the Christmas festivities in 1783, for instance, at a cost for £6 16s. 6d.[27] Inconsistencies in the account book entries make it difficult to determine the precise period of employment or the precise number of musicians employed on any occasion. Some musicians were paid on the night for musical services rendered while the services of others were retained for a number of nights and paid on a monthly or quarter-year basis.

Individual instrumentalists were also hired but there seems to have been a distinction between the more informal dances that an individual piper or fiddler played for and the larger invitational balls which required the services of a group. Individual musicians were more likely than a group to have been hired for a children's ball, a servants' ball or a harvest dance. However, a large-scale event might have required simultaneous music-making: an individual piper might have been found playing outdoors or in the servants' quarters while a group of fiddlers entertained guests of higher social rank in the drawing-rooms. In any case, the Castletown account books reveal that, until the 1780s, the musical services provided by individual pipers, like McDonald, and fiddlers, like Meehan and Higgins, were categorized alongside charity donations and other 'sundry' expenses. Entries in the tradesmen's receipts books from the 1780s reveal that individual musicians, such as James Cosgrove or Richard Crawley, were probably illiterate. Crawley, a fiddler whose name appears in the books between 1790 and 1800 for his regular 'attendance on dances at Castletown', always made a mark, as opposed to signing his name, for payments received.

Some of the amounts paid to musicians at Castletown included not only remuneration for musical services but also for travelling expenses. Again, inconsistent account book entries mean that this is not always revealed but in September 1782, for example, we find that £2 16s. 10½d. was expended 'to the fiddlers, and their chaise hire'.[28] Bands of musicians were hired for the lavish balls held at Castletown in the 1780s. Although the word 'band' might have simply signified a group of fiddlers, it was usually associated with a more structured ensemble comprising wind instrumentalists. It would not have been extraordinary for the Conollys to employ a band comprising French horns, for instance, as these were employed to entertain guests dining at Carton in the 1780s.[29] Moreover, wind instruments were becoming popular in an increasingly militarized social climate and dancing-masters like Aubry made a point of highlighting their usage in his non-domiciliary entertainments. The bands at Castletown in the late 1780s usually travelled from Dublin and appear to have been organized by literate men, who may or may not have been musicians themselves. In January 1788, for example, £5 13s. 9d. was paid to a man named Anthony Querny 'for music and chaise hire from Dublin to Castletown'.[30] Querny may have acted as the manager of the band and as a master-of-ceremonies, calling dances, at the Castletown ball.

Musicians were not generally hired at Castletown for musical concerts – they were usually hired to facilitate social dancing. Women staying at the house did, however, often provide music for the informal entertainment of close friends, as Mrs Gardiner did for the company in the long gallery in the 1770s. Domestic diversion, then, appears to have been the purpose of musical instruction for young ladies in the 18th century, as acknowledged by Louisa Conolly herself when learning music at Blackrock in 1768. Moreover, singing, playing or listening to music was considered an appropriate means of occupying the female mind and keeping in good spirits which, in turn, was believed to have positive corporeal effects.[31] Still, some women were clearly concerned with displaying 'taste' in their musical preferences, something which

music lessons would have enhanced. Louisa Conolly, as noted, was troubled
by her inability to understand serious instrumental or 'Italian' music as well
as she did the popular theatre songs. (This was probably why there were not
concerts of this sort held at Castletown.) Nonetheless, she dutifully attended
non-domiciliary concerts and operas even though she found these tiresome.
She took the young ladies in her care to hear 'music' at churches like St
Werburgh's in Dublin. They also attended subscription concerts at the main
assembly rooms in Dublin and London; Louisa paid for a life subscription of
£11 7s. 6d. to the Rotunda on behalf of Harriette Staples in 1788.[32] Whether
or not these girls had musical interest or ability, being seen to appreciate music
of quality was evidently another important aspect of elite female social
behaviour.

That the Staples girls were genuinely inclined towards music is evidenced
by the fact that when in London, the Conollys hired out musical instruments
for them. Although Thomas was no longer an MP in the English house of
commons and the Conollys were focused on life in Ireland, they continued
to visit relatives and friends in England during the 1780s and 1790s,
accompanied now by their young charges. The household account books show
that pianos and harpsichords were supplied by a number of prominent
London-based businesses. Once again, inconsistencies in the entries do not
always reveal the precise period of hire but it was probably on a monthly basis.
In the summer of 1783, for example, a pianoforte was hired from John
Pohlman at a total cost of 16s. That this instrument was actually used is borne
out by Louisa's complaint to her sister Emily that she was being distracted
from letter-writing by the girls 'playing upon the pianoforte, singing and
dancing, and making such a noise'.[33]

While staying at Castletown in February 1783, Emily's daughter Sophia
noted in her journal: 'I did get up rather earlier than usual and amused myself
playing two or three tunes Harriette [Staples] had brought me on the
harpsichord till breakfast'.[34] Sophia's statement points to the fact that the
Conollys owned a harpsichord at Castletown which was played by the young
ladies living in the house. It is not known who built or supplied the
harpsichord itself but the household account and tradesmen's receipt books
provide evidence of its maintenance. Inconsistencies in the entries do not
always reveal the number of times tuning and repairs occurred; some of the
sums paid suggest periodic maintenance. In addition, it is not entirely clear if
it was the named persons or their agents who actually performed the
maintenance on each occasion. Nonetheless, it can be said that the Conollys
patronized a number of prominent Dublin-based musical instrument-makers
including Mr William Gibson, Mrs Rachel Weber and Mr Thomas Kenny.[35]

In 1782, Gibson was paid 11s. 4½d. for tuning the harpsichord at Castletown
'sundry times'. Contemporary trade directories show that Gibson was a

prominent music-master, musical instrument-maker and music publisher located, at this time, at Grafton Street. Gibson's fee also included the tuning of a pianoforte at the Conolly's rented house on Merrion Street.[36] This instrument was also tuned by Rachel Weber, the Irish wife of the German organ-builder and harpsichord-maker Ferdinand Weber (1715–84), who carried on the renowned Weber business at Marlborough Street for some years after his death. Rachel Weber also tuned the harpsichord at Castletown, four times at a cost of 16s. 3d. each time.[37] The continual tuning of this harpsichord would denote consistent use. Between 1793 and 1800, Thomas Kenny, a pianoforte-maker at Mercer Street, seems to have had a contract for tuning and repairs to the Conollys' keyboard instruments at Castletown. The Conollys now also had a 'grand pianoforte', purchased in 1796 from John Broadwood and Son in London for the sum of £77 3s. 6d.[38] Significantly, the tradesmen's receipt books show that maintenance of these instruments continued right through the difficult years of the late 1790s until 1821, the year of Louisa Conolly's death, when she paid £8 2s. 'for tuning and buffing' of the Broadwood pianoforte.[39] This piano had been purchased for the education and entertainment of the most recent long-term resident at Castletown: Emily Napier (1783–1863).

Emily was the daughter of Louisa's sister Sarah by her second husband George Napier (1751–1804). After Emily's birth, the unhappily childless Louisa asked the Napiers to let her raise the child as her own. Sarah eventually agreed on the basis of the greater prospects offered to Emily by her wealthy, socially connected aunt.[40] While her parents eventually settled in Ireland and lived in nearby Celbridge, Emily Napier lived at Castletown from 1784 until Louisa's death in 1821. She clearly loved music and dancing and seems to have been exposed to plenty of it from a very young age. As early as 1785, Louisa Conolly reported to Sarah: 'she also loves dancing, and whenever the girls play upon the harpsichord she sets off and has a notion of turning her little arms over head'.[41] As well as providing evidence of the playing of the harpsichord at Castletown this suggests that the music being played was suitable for dancing.

There were also the lavish balls, which marked the zenith of sociability at Castletown in the late 1780s. As a 2-year-old, Emily Napier was often discovered 'trotting about' at these events, delighting everybody by 'holding her little petticoats to dance like the company'.[42] When she was eight years of age, Emily began music lessons with Harriette Staples' music-master, John Day, with whom she continued until the late 1790s. It seems to have been for her benefit that a harpsichord was hired, at a cost of £1 11s. 6d., while the Conollys were in London in 1791. The following year, £1 3s. was paid to Longman and Broderip, the English firm of music publishers and instrument makers, for the hire of a harpsichord at an agreed rate of 10s. 6d. per month. It was also in London that Emily appears to have taken her first dancing lessons. Her dancing-master was Mr Wilson and she was enrolled at his dancing academy at a cost of £1 1s. Wilson was an authority in the art of dancing and had, by 1809, authored two books on the subject: *Analysis of country-dancing* and *Treasures of Terpsichore*. Advertisements for his entertainments appeared on the front pages of London newspapers, along similar lines to those of Fontaine and Aubry in Dublin. Emily Napier took lessons with him for two months in the spring of 1792 at a cost of £2 2s.[43]

Back at Castletown, Emily took lessons with a dancing-master who appears to have been named Mr G. Grecco. She enrolled in June 1799 at the usual entrance-fee of £2 5s. 6d. and continued lessons with him into the early years of the 19th century. While little is known about Grecco, it appears from theatre advertisements in contemporary newspapers that he was an innovative choreographer of dances 'never performed in this kingdom'.[44] In the 1780s, both he and his dances regularly appeared in the interludes of various comic productions at the Smock Alley theatre. In 1791, a Mr Grecco called the dances as the master-of-ceremonies at a large ball held at Carton to mark the christening of Augustus Frederick FitzGerald (1791–1874), afterwards the 3rd duke of Leinster.[45]

Despite the civil unrest and decline of sociability at Castletown in the 1790s, Louisa Conolly tried to maintain a sense of normality for Emily Napier. Musicians continued to be hired for small parties and dances. In 1796, for instance, a John Tracy was paid £8 10s. 7d. for 'two nights music and chaise hire' in January and £3 8s. 3d. for one night in December.[46] This may have been the musician who married in 1779 and was noted as living at Fishamble Street in Dublin.[47] It may also have been the man who collaborated with the music seller and publisher, Bartlett Cooke, to produce *Tracy's selection of the present favorite country dances* in the 1790s.[48] Like many printed country dance collections, this publication contained notated music and instructions for dancing to it. Cooke collaborated on similar collections with Mr Fontaine, which hints that Tracy may have also been a dancing-master, or a master-of-ceremonies paid to organize the musicians for and call the dances at a ball. Individual musicians also continued to be hired at Castletown; in January 1796, for instance, James Cosgrove, was paid the sum of £5 13s. 9d., the receipt for which he made a mark rather than a signature.[49] The presence of a garrison at the house provided occasions for impromptu musical activity as, on 15 August 1797, when 'one of the soldiers' was given 5s. 5d. by the Conollys 'for playing the fiddle'.[50]

There had been talk at Castletown as early as 1795 of 'an union with England', something which Louisa and Thomas hoped '*never* to see'.[51] Yet, Thomas supported the union between Ireland and Great Britain as proposed by Robert Stewart (1769–1822), Viscount Castlereagh. Stewart was the chief secretary in Ireland from 1799 to 1801 and Thomas's nephew by marriage having wed Lady Amelia Anne Hobart (1772–1829) in 1796. In 1800, some months before the union came into effect, Thomas retired from politics. Visitors continued to be entertained at Castletown even though many of the occasions for music and dancing were for the entertainment of Emily Napier. In April 1800, a literate fiddler, Hugh Browne, was hired to play for two nights at a cost of £1 2s. 9d. In August, the first reference to a harper appears in the household account books when a literate man, Henry Gieseler, was paid £3 8s. 3d. for 'music, and playing on the harp at the dances in Castletown'.[52] This is not to say that harpers were not among the various anonymous musicians who rendered musical services over the years. Louisa's personal accounts reveal that she occasionally patronized harpers on her travels throughout the 1770s, with small sums of 1s. 1d., 2s. 8½d. and 11s. 4½d.[53] Another literate musician, Patrick Gallaher, was also paid for 'playing at the dances in Castletown' in August 1800, so either Gieseler and Gallaher played together at the same dances or played simultaneously for different groups of people.

After 1800, Thomas Conolly became generally depressed and his health declined. As well as the family awkwardness and divided loyalties which surfaced in 1798, he was in great debt and embroiled in a legal dispute with his sisters regarding settlements owed to them.[54] Louisa, on the other hand, came back to prominence in Dublin society and, Thomas being on good terms with the government, was back at Dublin Castle. Owing to the resignation of the lord lieutenant, Charles Cornwallis (1738–1805), the 1st Marquis Cornwallis, it was Louisa who 'did the honours of lady lieutenant' at a ball held at the Castle in March 1801.[55] She also tried to reinvigorate sociability at Castletown. In August 1802, she told her niece Sophia FitzGerald that she had recently 'had all the grand folks' there and had thrown them 'a little dance ... that I mean should serve them till X'mas'.[56] True to her word, Louisa held another ball on 31 December 1802 and hired two fiddlers for it at a cost of 16s. 9½d.[57] Little is known about music and dancing at Castletown after Thomas's death in 1803 apart from the fact that these activities continued to function in the social lives of the women who lived there.

Although music was largely considered as a playful or perfunctory diversion, it was, nonetheless, an effective agent of cultural transfer. Women shared printed music sheets and copied from these into small ruled manuscript music books. That this occurred at Castletown would appear to be borne out by the existence of just such a copy-book.[58] Currently in private ownership, the small volume bears the title 'Manuscript music' and contains over 40 short pieces of music transcribed, primarily in ink, by a number of different hands. What links the book with Castletown is the inscription, 'Castletown Aug. 1815', written in ink directly after the final piece titled 'Mr Temple's Waltz'. The watermark on the paper bears the date 1806 which indicates that the transcriptions were done sometime between then and 1815. The transcriptions appear to be for a keyboard instrument and comprise dances such as reels, rondos and waltzes. Many of the waltzes are untitled except for the designations 'quick' and 'slow' or an attribution to Mozart. Titled transcriptions include: 'Och Lieber Augustin', 'Saltarello', 'Miss Johnston's Reel', 'Lady Mary Ramsay', 'The Sylph', 'Morgiana in Ireland', 'The Fairy Dance', 'Bolare Waltz', 'The Russian Dance', 'Danish Waltz', 'The Darmstadt Waltz', 'Polish Rondo' and 'Duke of Leinster's Sarabande'. These titles suggest both local and international influences but it is difficult to establish if the book belonged to a member of the Conolly family, to somebody teaching or playing the music at Castletown, or to somebody who jotted down the pieces while visiting Castletown.

One of the persons most likely to have been connected with the book was Emily Napier. By the summer of 1815, she had been exposed to the very latest fashions in music and dancing at the highest levels of European society. She had, for instance, accompanied Louisa Conolly on a visit to Harriette (Staples) Trench in The Hague in the spring and summer of 1814. Their visit to this social centre in the newly united kingdom of the Netherlands followed on the cessation of European hostilities after the fall of Napoleonic France. Harriette's husband, Lord Clancarty, was the British ambassador to and a personal friend of the regent, Prince William of Orange-Nassau (1772–1843). At The Hague, Emily and Louisa were engaged in a busy round of social activities, which included dancing at lavish balls. In July 1814, they attended a ball held in honour of the Russian emperor, Alexander I (1777–1825), at which Emily was chosen by the emperor as one of his dancing partners.[59] Louisa told her sister Sarah: 'when the fiddles began the country dances, he marched straight off [to] where Emily was, took hold of her hands and brought her out to dance'.[60] Among the dances performed at the ball was the waltz, a partner-dance which was well in vogue on the Continent at this time. Perhaps some of the waltz tunes transcribed in the 'Castletown' manuscript music book, such as 'The Darmstadt Waltz', related to those performed at The Hague in 1814. From the long descriptions of the ball provided by Emily and Louisa to relatives and friends, it seems that they were both familiar with the waltz but were struck by a dance, known as a polonaise, which they had never witnessed before. The polonaise was a stately dance of Polish origin but Louisa thought that, while it had 'a pretty tune', it looked more like walking than dancing. She told Sarah: 'dancing it is not, for the gentlemen all step out with a lady and most composedly walk in a circle round the room and lead out to as many rooms as are opened and then return to the room'.[61] It is tempting to conclude that this exposure to new forms of music and dancing had a bearing on whatever activity occurred at Castletown, in the final years of the life of Lady Louisa Augusta Conolly.

By the terms of Thomas Conolly's will, Castletown was left to Louisa during her lifetime and thereafter to the family of Louisa and Thomas Pakenham. Consequently, on Louisa Conolly's death in 1821, the estate devolved on Colonel Edward Michael Pakenham (1786–1848), who assumed, not only the Conolly name and arms, but Castletown's legacy of society, comfort, friendship, hospitality and entertainment.

Conclusion

Life at Castletown in the late 18th and early 19th centuries was entirely fashioned by the connections, commitments and experiences of Thomas and Louisa Conolly. The Conollys' long-established relationship with Dublin Castle was particularly significant. The viceroyalty of Buckinghamshire, Thomas's brother by marriage, marked the beginning of a high period of sociability and entertainment at Castletown that lasted until the 1790s. The decline of Castletown as the centre of sociability and entertainment in Ireland, however, coincided with a decline in relations with Dublin Castle. Nonetheless, Castletown was always an engaging place for relatives, friends, neighbours, political peers, business associates and invited guests to meet to discuss political developments, to gossip about the latest scandal, to negotiate patronage, to exhibit the latest in fashionable dress, and to enable the marriage market. Louisa Conolly had succeeded in her aim to transform Castletown from a place of formal processionality to a fashionable place of domiciliary sociability capable, when necessary, of facilitating hundreds of people. Music and dancing were significant agents of this sociability. However, music functioned to facilitate social dancing and rarely featured as an entertainment in its own right. Dancing was an integral aspect of social life and prominent dancing-masters were employed by the Conollys to provide lessons in appropriate social behaviour as well as the requisite dance steps. Exposure to the latest fashions in dancing was provided at Dublin Castle as well as regular trips to London and other cities, further afield.

Music and dancing also functioned at Castletown in terms of the social education of members of the extended Conolly family. Music-masters were hired for the instruction of the young females resident in the house, who practised music informally for their own amusement. Musical influences were provided by subscription concerts and benefit performances attended at non-domiciliary venues such as assembly rooms and theatres. The keyboard instruments owned at Castletown were consistently utilized, the Conollys patronizing some of the leading instrument-makers in Dublin for their maintenance. The scholarly examination of music and dancing, as aspects of domiciliary sociability, entertainment and, indeed, education, provides a useful framework for investigating the lives, pastimes, concerns, tastes, fashions and aspirations of the people who lived and worked at a house like Castletown. It is hoped that the significance and, indeed, necessity of such studies, has been demonstrated, particularly for the perspectives it provides on the form, function and furnishing of an Irish country house.

Notes

Punctuation and spellings have been modernized and the use of capital letters normalized where quotations have been taken from original letters, journals, account books and tradesmen's receipt books.

ABBREVIATIONS

BP   Bunbury Papers
CEDL   *Correspondence of Emily, Duchess of Leinster,* ed. Brian Fitzgerald 3 vols (Dublin, 1949, 1953, 1957)
CL   Conolly Letters
CNP   Conolly-Napier Papers
CP   Castletown Papers
FJ   *Freeman's Journal*
HMC   Historical Manuscripts Commission
IAA   Irish Architectural Archive, Dublin
ITMA   Irish Traditional Music Archive, Dublin
LFCP   Lennox/FitzGerald/Campbell Papers
NLI   National Library of Ireland, Dublin
PRONI   Public Record Office of Northern Ireland, Belfast
QBIGS   *Quarterly Bulletin of the Irish Georgian Society*
SP   Strutt Papers
TCD   Trinity College Dublin

INTRODUCTION

1 See Patrick Walsh, *The making of the Protestant ascendancy: the life of William Conolly, 1662–1729* (Woodbridge, 2010).

2 Patrick Walsh, 'Biography and the meaning of an Irish country house: William Conolly and Castletown' in Terence Dooley & Christopher Ridgway (eds), *The Irish country house: its past, present and future* (Dublin, 2011), p. 28.

3 See Patrick Walsh, 'The career of William Conolly, 1689–1729' (PhD thesis, TCD, 2007), ch. 1.

4 Walsh, 'Biography and the meaning of an Irish country house', pp 28–35.

5 The term 'domiciliary sociability' is used by Gillian Russell in her *Women, sociability and theatre in Georgian London* (Cambridge, 2007), p. 11.

6 For contemporary English examples see Elaine Chalus, '"To serve my friends": women and political patronage in 18th-century England', in Amanda Vickery (ed.), *Women, privilege and power: British politics, 1750 to the present* (Stanford, 2001), pp 57–88.

7 Toby Barnard, *Making the grand figure: lives and possessions in Ireland, 1641–1770* (New Haven, 2004), pp 71–80.

8 Brian Boydell, 'Music, 1700–1850' in T.W. Moody & W.E. Vaughan (eds), *A new history of Ireland, iv: 18th-century Ireland 1691–1800* (Oxford, 1986), p. 570; pp 579–80.

9 Barnard, *Making the grand figure*, pp 17–18.

10 Toby Barnard, *Irish protestant ascents and descents, 1641–1770* (Dublin, 2004), pp 280–4.

11 Joseph Robins, *Champagne and silver buckles: the viceregal court and Dublin Castle* (Dublin, 2001), p. 46.

12 Frances Rust, *Dance in society* (London, 1969), pp 59–60.

13 Stephen Philpot, *An essay on the advantage of a polite education joined with a learned one* (London, 1746), pp 27–28; 88–115.

14 Toby Barnard, *Irish protestant ascents,* p. 284.

15 Elizabeth Gibson, 'Owen Swiney and the Italian opera in London', *Musical Times*, 125:1692 (Feb. 1984), 82–6.

16 Brian Fitzgerald, *Lady Louisa Conolly, 1743–1821: an Anglo-Irish biography* (London, 1950), p. 17.

17 Boydell, 'Music, 1700–1850', pp 583–4.

18 For details on some of these see Patrick Walsh & A.P.W. Malcomson, *The Conolly archive* (Dublin, 2010).

19 Some of these include: Desmond FitzGerald, 'New light on Castletown, Co. Kildare', *QBIGS*, 8:1 (1965), 3–9; Lena Boylan, 'The Conollys of Castletown', *QBIGS*, 11:4 (1968), 1–46; Maurice Craig & Desmond Guinness, 'Castletown, Co. Kildare', *Country Life*, 145:3760 (27 March 1969), 722–6; Christopher Moore, 'Lady Louisa Conolly: mistress of Castletown, 1759–1821' in Jane Fenlon, Nicola Figgis & Catherine Marshall (eds), *New perspectives: studies in art history in honour of Anne Crookshank* (Dublin, 1987), pp 123–41; David Griffin, 'Castletown, Co. Kildare: the contribution of James, 1st duke of Leinster', *Irish Architectural and Decorative Studies*, 1 (1998), 120–46; Patrick Walsh, *Castletown* (Dublin, 2007).

1. MUSIC AND DANCING IN THE SOCIAL MILIEU OF THE CONOLLYS

1 C. Fox to E. FitzGerald, 27 Mar. 1759, *CEDL*, i, pp 204–5.

2 L. Conolly to E. FitzGerald, 10 Apr. 1759, *CEDL*, iii, p. 7.

3 L. Conolly to E. FitzGerald, 1 May 1759, *CEDL*, iii, pp 17–18.

4 J. FitzGerald to E. FitzGerald, 8 May 1759, *CEDL*, i, p. 78.

5 H. Walpole to G. Montagu, 1 May 1759, in *The letters of Horace Walpole, earl of Orford* (4 vols, London, 1840), ii, p. 486.

6 L. Conolly to E. FitzGerald, 28 May 1759, *CEDL*, iii, p. 20.

7 See, for example, Anon., *An address to persons of fashion, containing some particulars relating to balls …* (3rd ed., London, 1761).

8 C. Fox to E. FitzGerald, 18 Aug. 1759, *CEDL*, i, p. 250.

9 The most enduring of these was John Playford's *The English dancing master or plaine and basic rules of country dances* (London, 1651), new editions of which were published until 1728.

10 Rust, *Dance in society*, pp 56–7; p. 61.

11 See, for example, John & William Neal, *A choice collection of country dances* (Dublin, c.1726).

12 Helen Brennan, *The story of Irish dance* (Dingle, 1999), pp 16–20; 93–4; Mary Friel, *Dancing as a social pastime in the south-east of Ireland, 1800–1897* (Dublin, 2004), pp 44–5.

13 'A.D.', *Country-dancing made plain and easy* (London, 1764), pp 19–21.

14 Fitzgerald, *Lady Louisa Conolly*, pp 46–9; 51–4.

15 L. Conolly to S. Lennox, 15 Dec. 1760 (IAA, CL, 94/136/1).

16 L. Conolly to S. Lennox, 30 Dec. 1760 (IAA, CL, 94/136/1).

17 L. Conolly to S. Lennox, 15 Dec. 1760 (IAA, CL, 94/136/1).

18 L. Conolly to S. Lennox, 6, 25 Apr. 1761 (IAA, CL, 94/136/1).

19 L. Conolly to S. Lennox, 26 Jan. 1762 (IAA, CL, 94/136/1).

20 Peter Clark, *British clubs and societies, 1580–1800* (Oxford, 2002), p. 192.

21 L. Conolly to S. Bunbury, 30 Dec. 1762 (IAA, CL, 94/136/1).

22 L. Conolly to S. Bunbury, 29 Jan. 1767 (IAA, CL, 94/136/1).

23 L. Conolly to S. Bunbury, 2 Feb. 1768 (IAA, CL, 94/136/1).

24 Robins, *Champagne and silver buckles*, p. 35; 56–7.

25 M. Clarke (agent) to T. Conolly, 1 June 1765 (NLI MS 41,341/3).

26 L. Conolly to S. Bunbury, 2 Feb. 1768 (IAA, CL, 94/136/1).

27 L. Conolly to S. Bunbury, 5 Feb. 1768 (IAA, CL, 94/136/1).

28 L. Conolly to S. Bunbury, 14 Feb. 1768 (IAA, CL, 94/136/1).

29 L. Conolly to S. Bunbury, 22 Feb. 1768 (IAA, CL, 94/136/1).

30 L. Conolly to S. Bunbury, 26 Apr., 8 May 1768 (IAA, CL, 94/136/1).

31 *The Monthly Magazine, or British Register*, 5 (1798), 550.

32 Constantia Maxwell, *Country and town in Ireland under the Georges* (revised ed., Dundalk, 1949), p. 251.

33 Rust, *Dance in society*, p. 61.

34 See Brian Boydell, *Rotunda music in 18th-century Dublin* (Dublin, 1992).

35 R. Lewis, *The Dublin guide: or, A description of the city of Dublin and the most remarkable places within fifteen miles* (Dublin, 1787), pp 276–7.

36 L. Conolly to S. Bunbury, 5 Feb. 1768 (IAA, CL, 94/136/1).

37 L. Conolly to S. Bunbury, 3 May 1768 (IAA, CL, 94/136/1).

38 *FJ*, 6 May 1777.

39 Mark Girouard, *Life in an English country house: a social and architectural history* (New Haven, 1978), p. 194.

40 Christopher Morash, *A history of Irish theatre, 1601–2000* (Cambridge, 2002), pp 13–14; 28; 50. Maxwell, *Country and town*, pp 185–212.

41 Fitzgerald, *Lady Louisa Conolly*, p. 32.

42 L. Conolly to S. Lennox, 13 Feb. 1762 (IAA, CL, 94/136/1).

43 E. FitzGerald to J. FitzGerald, 16 Dec 1762, *CEDL*, i, pp 155–6.

44 L. Conolly to S. Bunbury, 29 Jan. 1767 (IAA, CL, 94/136/1).

45 Harry White, *The keeper's recital: music and cultural history in Ireland, 1770–1970* (Cork, 1998), pp 27–8.

46 Personal account book of L. Conolly, 1766–75 (TCD, MS 3966).

47 Boydell, 'Music, 1700–1850', pp 586–7.

48 T.J. Walsh, *Opera in Dublin, 1705–1797: the social scene* (Dublin, 1973).

49 Account book (TCD, MS 3966).

50 L. Conolly to S. Bunbury, 13 Nov. 1771 (IAA, CL, 94/136/1).

51 Lewis, *The Dublin guide*, pp 61–2.

52 L. Conolly to S. Bunbury, 7 July 1768 (IAA, CL, 94/136/1).

53 Account book (TCD, MS 3966).

54 Philip Coggin, '"This easy and agreable instrument": a history of the English guittar', *Early Music*, 15:2 (1987), 204–18.

55 L. Conolly to S. Bunbury, 2 Aug. 1768 (IAA, CL, 94/136/1).

56 See, for example, J. Pemberton, *A mechanical essay on singing, musick and dancing* (London, 1727).

57 L. Conolly to S. Lennox, 25 Apr. 1761 (IAA, CL, 94/136/1).

58 L. Conolly to S. FitzGerald, 2 Aug. 1802 (NLI, LFCP, MS 35,004/5).

59 L. Conolly to S. Bunbury, 22 Aug. 1768 (IAA, CL, 94/136/1).

60 L. Conolly to E. FitzGerald, 10 Feb. 1770, *CEDL*, iii, pp 41–2.

61 Russell, *Women, sociability and theatre*, pp 17–37.

62 James Peller Malcolm, *Anecdotes of the manners and customs of London during the 18th century* (London, 1810), pp 272–5.

63 L. Conolly to E. FitzGerald, 28 Feb. 1770, *CEDL*, iii, pp 48–9.

64 L. Conolly to E. FitzGerald, 15 Jan. 1773, *CEDL*, iii, pp 63–4.

65 Fitzgerald, *Lady Louisa Conolly*, pp 15–6.

66 See account book (TCD, MS 3966).

67 L. Conolly to S. Bunbury, 9 Mar. 1771 (IAA, CL, 94/136/1); Account book of L. Conolly (TCD, MS 3966).

68 L. Conolly to E. FitzGerald, 30 Jan. 1773, *CEDL*, iii, p. 69.

69 Account book (TCD, MS 3966).

70 Fitzgerald, *Lady Louisa Conolly*, pp 59–61.

71 Boydell, 'Music, 1700–1850', p. 568; White, *The keeper's recital*, pp 14–27.

72 C. Fox to E. FitzGerald, 18 May 1765, *CEDL*, i, p. 426.

73 L. Conolly to E. Ogilvie, 17 Feb. 1775, *CEDL*, iii, p. 119.

2. OCCASIONS FOR MUSIC AND DANCING AT CASTLETOWN

1 L. Conolly to S. Lennox, n.d. [May 1762] (IAA, CL, 94/136/1).

2 Girouard, *Life in an English country house*, pp 158–194; Moore, 'Lady Louisa Conolly', pp 123–41.

3 J. FitzGerald to E. FitzGerald, 10 June 1766 (PRONI, SP, T3092/1/4).

4 L. Conolly to S. Bunbury, 22 Feb. 1768 (IAA, CL, 94/136/1).

5 See Ruth Johnstone, 'Revisiting the print room' (PhD thesis, Royal Melbourne Institute of Technology University, Melbourne, 2004; extracts available at the IAA).

6 L. Conolly to S. Lennox, 6 Apr. 1761 (IAA, CL, 94/136/1).

7 Fitzgerald, *Lady Louisa Conolly*, pp 55–8.

8 L. Conolly to S. Lennox, 22 May 1762 (IAA, CL, 94/136/1).

9 Girouard, *Life in an English country house*, p. 232.

10 L. Conolly to S. Bunbury, 30 Dec. 1762 (IAA, CL, 94/136/1).

11 L. Conolly to E. Ogilvie, 9 Oct 1774, *CEDL*, iii, p. 91.

12 L. Conolly to S. Bunbury, 5 May 1767 (IAA, CL, 94/136/1).

13 Girouard, *Life in an English country house*, p. 233.

14 L. Conolly to S. Bunbury, 17 Sept. 1771 (IAA, CL, 94/136/1).

15 L. Conolly to E. Ogilvie, 7 Dec. 1775, *CEDL*, iii, p. 169.

16 Fitzgerald, *Lady Louisa Conolly*, pp 98–9.

17 *Gleanings from an old portfolio containing some correspondence between Lady Louisa Stuart and her sister Caroline, Countess of Portarlington*, ed. Mrs Godfrey Clark (2 vols, Edinburgh, 1895), i, p. 83.

18 Fitzgerald, *Lady Louisa Conolly*, pp 55–8.

19 *The private theatre of Kilkenny with introductory observations on other private theatres before it was opened* (privately published, 1825), pp 1–2.

20 *An asylum for fugitive pieces in prose and verse, not in any other collection: with several pieces never before published, iii*, printed for J. Debrett (London, 1799), p. 275.

21 L. Conolly to E. Ogilvie, 14 Dec. 1775, 5 Jan. 1776, *CEDL*, iii, pp 169–81.

22 *The private theatre of Kilkenny*, pp 1–2; L. Conolly to S. Lennox, 30 Dec. 1760 (IAA, CL, 94/136/1).

23 L. Conolly to S. Bunbury, 7 Sept. 1767 (IAA, CL, 94/136/1).

24 Personal account book of T. Conolly, 1767–70 (TCD, MS 3964).

25 L. Conolly to S. Bunbury, 5 May 1767 (IAA, CL, 94/136/1).

26 Moore, 'Lady Louisa Conolly', pp 131–2.

27 L. Conolly to S. Bunbury, 14, 30 Aug. 1772 (IAA, CL, 94/136/1).

28 Household account book, 1767–77 (TCD, MS 3953).

29 L. Conolly to S. Bunbury, 14, 30 Aug. 1772 (IAA, CL, 94/136/1).

30 Rust, *Dance in society*, pp 60–1.

31 L. Conolly to S. Bunbury, 8 Dec. 1771 (IAA, CL, 94/136/1).

32 L. Conolly to S. Bunbury, 29 Jan. 1772 (IAA, CL, 94/136/1).

33 L. Conolly to S. Bunbury, 8 Dec. 1771 (IAA, CL, 94/136/1).

34 L. Conolly to S. Bunbury, 15 Nov. 1767 (IAA, CL, 94/136/1); Account book of L. Conolly (TCD, MS 3966).

35 L. Conolly to T. Conolly, 3 Apr. 1772 (IAA, CL, 94/136/1).

36 *A select collection of the most admired songs, duetts &c from operas in the highest esteem and from other works in Italian, English, French, Scotch, Irish &c&c in three books* (Edinburgh, n.d.).

37 L. Conolly to S. Bunbury, 29 Jan. 1772 (IAA, CL, 94/136/1).

38 Arthur Young, *A tour in Ireland, 1776–1779*, ed. A.W. Hutton (2 vols, Shannon, 1970), ii, p. 147; p. 366.

39 L. Conolly to S. Bunbury, 9 Aug. 1768 (IAA, CL, 94/136/1).

40 Account book (TCD, MS 3953).

41 See Maxwell, *Country and town*, pp 183–4.

42 Household account book of sundry expenses, 1796–1802 (IAA, CP, 97/84/J/11).

43 Girouard, *Life in an English country house*, pp 214–18.

44 Fitzgerald, *Lady Louisa Conolly*, p. 4.

45 Household account book, 1778–88 (TCD, MS 3955).

46 Robins, *Champagne and silver buckles*, p. 47.

47 L. Conolly to E. Ogilvie, 5 Jan. 1776, *CEDL*, iii, p. 181.

48 L. Conolly to E. Ogilvie, 11 July 1776, *CEDL*, iii, p. 210.

49 L. Conolly to S. Bunbury, 8 Oct. 1777 (IAA, CL, 94/136/1).

50 Personal account book of T. Conolly, 1775–84 (TCD, MS 3965).

51 L. Conolly to E. Ogilvie, 21 Dec. 1776, *CEDL*, iii, p. 243.

52 L. Conolly to E. Ogilvie, 28 Jan. 1777, *CEDL*, iii, pp 248–50.

53 Account book (TCD, MS 3965).
54 L. Conolly to S. Bunbury, 31 Aug. 1777 (IAA, CL, 94/136/2).
55 L. Conolly to E. Ogilvie, 28 Jan. 1777, *CEDL*, iii, pp 248–9.
56 L. Conolly to E. Ogilvie, 28 Nov. 1777, *CEDL*, iii, p. 258.
57 Michael Kelly, *Reminiscences*, ed. R. Fiske (London, 1975), pp 7–10.
58 L. Conolly to E. Ogilvie, 28 Nov. 1777, *CEDL*, iii, p. 258.
59 L. Conolly to S. Bunbury, 24 May 1778 (IAA, CL, 94/136/2).
60 L. Conolly to E. Ogilvie, 24 July 1778, *CEDL*, iii, p. 304.
61 Account book (TCD, MS 3955).
62 L. Conolly to E. Ogilvie, 24 July, 30 Aug., 6 Sept. 1778, *CEDL*, iii, pp 304–11.
63 L. Conolly to S. Bunbury, n.d. 1781 (IAA, CL, 94/136/2).
64 L. Conolly to S. Bunbury, 25 Oct. 1777 (IAA, CL, 94/136/2).
65 L. Conolly to S. Bunbury, 13 Aug. 1762 (IAA, CL, 94/136/1).
66 Thomas Campbell, *A philosophical survey of the south of Ireland* (Dublin, 1778), p. 55.
67 T. Conolly to J. Hobart, 13 Jan 1781, in HMC, *Report on the manuscripts of the marquis of Lothian preserved at Blickling Hall, Norfolk* (London, 1905), pp 380–1.
68 L. Conolly to S. Napier, 26 Dec. 1782 (PRONI, BP, T3795/1/113).
69 *FJ*, 14 Oct. 1779.
70 Account book (TCD, MS 3955); Tradesmen's receipt book, 1778–1785 (TCD, MS 3939).
71 Account book (TCD, MS 3955).
72 See *FJ*, 30 June 1781 for detailed choreography of a military review at Bellewstown
73 Household account book, 1786–90 (TCD, MS 3956); Tradesmen's receipt book, 1778–1785 (TCD, MS 3940).
74 Servants' wages book, 1785–96 (TCD, MS 3943).
75 Lewis, *The Dublin guide*, pp 87–8.
76 L. Conolly to E. Ogilvie, 10 Dec. 1786, *CEDL*, iii, pp 390–1.
77 L. Conolly to S. Napier, 17 June 1784 (PRONI, BP, T3795/1/121).
78 L. Conolly to E. Ogilvie, 3, 10, 17 Dec. 1786, *CEDL*, iii, pp 387–93.
79 L. Conolly to S. Napier, 26 Dec. 1782 (PRONI, BP, T3795/1/113).
80 L. Conolly to E. Ogilvie, 3, 10, 17 Dec. 1786, *CEDL*, iii, pp 387–93.
81 Cited in Fitzgerald, *Lady Louisa Conolly*, p. 148.
82 Account books (TCD, MS 3955–6); Tradesmen's receipts (TCD, MS 3940).
83 L. Conolly to E. Ogilvie, 4 Jan. 1788, *CEDL*, iii, p. 413.
84 Account books (TCD, MS 3955–6); Tradesmen's receipts (TCD, MS 3940).
85 Fitzgerald, *Lady Louisa Conolly*, pp 150–4.
86 Account book (TCD, MS 3955–6).
87 Walsh & Malcomson, *The Conolly archive*, xvi–xvii.
88 Oracle and Public Advertiser, 30 June 1795.
89 L. Conolly to F. Jeffreys, 4 June 1795 [draft] (IAA, CL, 94/136/2).
90 F. Jeffreys to L. Conolly, 6 June 1795; L. Conolly to F. Jeffreys, 7 June 1795 (NLI, CNP, MS 34,922/22–23).
91 L. Conolly to T. Conolly, 19–20 July 1795 (NLI, CNP, MS 40,242/11).
92 L. Conolly to C. Lennox, 18 June 1798 (NLI, CNP, MS 34,922/9).

3. MASTERS, MUSICIANS AND MUSIC TRADESMEN

1 L. Conolly to S. Bunbury, 9 Sept. 1771 (IAA, CL, 94/136/1).
2 L. Conolly to S. Bunbury, 15 July 1777 (IAA, CL, 94/136/2).
3 L. Conolly to S. Bunbury, 18 June, 24 July, 7, 13, 20 Aug., 9 Sept. 1771 (IAA, CL, 94/136/1).
4 L. Conolly to S. Napier, 24 July 1782 (PRONI, BP, T3795/1/90).
5 L. Conolly to E. Ogilvie, 29 Nov. 1775, *CEDL*, iii, pp 163–4.
6 L. Conolly to S. Napier, 17 June 1784 (PRONI, BP, T3795/1/90).
7 Account books (TCD, MS 3955–6); Tradesmen's receipts (TCD, MS 3939–41).
8 L. Conolly to S. Napier, 24 July 1782 (PRONI, BP, T3795/1/90).
9 *FJ*, 23 May 1789.
10 Ibid.
11 L. Conolly to S. Napier, 7 Sept. 1782 (PRONI, BP, T3795/1/97).

12 Account book (TCD, MS 3955).
13 Journal entry, 28 Feb. 1783 (NLI, LFCP MS 35,012/1).
14 Journal entry, 10 Mar. 1783 (NLI, LFCP MS 35,012/1).
15 L. Conolly to S. Napier, 9 Oct. 1783 (PRONI, BP, T 3795/1/117).
16 L. Conolly to E. Ogilvie, 29 Oct., 2 Nov. 1783, *CEDL*, iii, pp 373–5.
17 L. Conolly to S. FitzGerald, 2 Aug. 1802 (NLI, LFCP, MS 35,004/5).
18 E. Bellamont to L. FitzGerald, 23 Oct. 1787 (PRONI, SP, T 3092/3/13).
19 FJ, 27 Mar. 1788.
20 Account books (TCD, MS 3955–6); Tradesmen's receipts (TCD, MS 3940).
21 L. Conolly to E. Ogilvie, 3 Dec. 1786, *CEDL*, iii, p. 387.
22 L. Conolly to E. Ogilvie, 17 Dec. 1786, *CEDL*, iii, p. 393.
23 Account book (TCD, MS 3954)
24 Account books (TCD, MS 3955–6); Tradesmen's receipts (TCD, MS 3939–41).
25 Account book (TCD, MS 3955); Tradesmen's receipts (TCD, MS 3939).
26 FJ, 10 Apr. 1816.
27 Account book (TCD, MS 3955).
28 Ibid.
29 Brian FitzGerald, *Emily, Duchess of Leinster* (London, 1949), pp 165–6.
30 Account books (TCD, MS 3955–6); Tradesmen's receipts (TCD, MS 3940).
31 Pemberton, *A mechanical essay*, passim.
32 Account books (TCD, MS 3955–6).
33 L. Conolly to E. Ogilvie, 29 Oct., 19 June 1783, *CEDL*, iii, p. 359.
34 Journal entry, 19 Feb. 1783 (NLI, LFCP MS 35,012/1).
35 Account books (TCD, MS 3955–7); Tradesmen's receipts (TCD, MS 3939–41).
36 Account book (TCD, MS 3955); Tradesmen's receipts (TCD, MS 3939).
37 Account book (TCD, MS 3955–6); Tradesmen's receipts (TCD, MS 3940).
38 L. Conolly to T. Conolly, 27 Dec. 1796 (IAA, CL, 94/136/2).
39 Account book (TCD, MS 3957).
40 Stella Tillyard, *Aristocrats: Caroline, Emily, Louisa and Sarah Lennox, 1740–1832* (London, 1994), p. 349.
41 L. Conolly to S. Napier, 2 Feb. 1785 (IAA, CL, 94/136/2).
42 L. Conolly to S. Napier, 6 Jan. 1785 (IAA, CL, 94/136/2).
43 Account book (TCD, MS 3954).
44 FJ, 26 Mar. 1785.
45 M. FitzGerald to C. Burgh, 26 Dec. 1791 (NLI, MS 41, 552/32).
46 Tradesmen's receipts (TCD, MS 3941).
47 FJ, 10 June 1779.
48 I am grateful to Mr Nicholas Carolan, Director, ITMA, for this reference (ITMA Ref: 28896-BK).
49 Tradesmen's receipts (TCD, MS 3941).
50 Account book (IAA, CP, 97/84/J/11).
51 L. Conolly to T. Conolly, 16 June 1795 (NLI, CNP, MS 40,242/8).
52 Tradesmen's receipts (TCD, MS 3941).
53 Account book (TCD, MS 3966).
54 Walsh & Malcomson, *The Conolly archive*, xviii.
55 *Morning Post and Gazetteer*, 5 Mar. 1801.
56 L. Conolly to S. FitzGerald, 2 Aug. 1802 (NLI, LFCP, MS 35,004/5).
57 Account book (IAA, CP, 97/84/J/11).
58 I am grateful to Mr Finian Corley for allowing me to examine this manuscript music book in his possession.
59 E. Napier to A. Staples, 2 July 1814 (NLI, MS 40,242/7).
60 L. Conolly to S. Napier, 5 July 1814 (PRONI, BP, T 3795/1/174).
61 Ibid.